Greg Laurie
marriage + connections

Tyndale House Publishers, Inc.
WHEATON, ILLINOIS

Visit Tyndale's exciting Web site at www.tyndale.com

Marriage Connections

Copyright © 2002 by Greg Laurie. All rights reserved.

Cover photograph copyright © 2002 by Chuck Keeler Jr./Corbis Images. All rights reserved.

Designed by Cathy Bergstrom

Edited by Dave Lindstedt

Library of Congress Cataloging-in-Publication Data

Laurie, Greg.
  Marriage connections / Greg Laurie.
    p. cm.
  Includes bibliographical references (p.) and index.
   ISBN 0-8423-5356-9
   1. Spouses—Prayer-books and devotions—English. 2. Marriage—Religious aspects—Christianity. I. Title.
BV4596.M3L39 2002
242'.644—dc21   2002009180

Printed in the United States of America

06 05 04 03 02
6   5   4   3   2   1

contents

time for a Refill

Do not get drunk on wine, which leads to debauchery. Instead, be filled with the Spirit. EPHESIANS 5:18

I HEARD A STORY once of a man who purchased a new car, drove it around for a week, then returned it to the dealer, demanding his money back and claiming the car to be a lemon.

"What's wrong with it?" the car dealer asked. "It seemed fine when you drove it off the lot."

"How about the fact that it doesn't run?" the man replied in frustration. To prove his point, he got in the car, put the key in the ignition and turned it. The car just sat there. No rumble of the engine. Nothing.

Suddenly the dealer noticed a little red light shining on the dashboard. He asked the angry customer, "Have you been to a gas station?"

"A gas station?" the man said. "No. What's that?"

"It's a place where you fill your car up with gas," explained the dealer. "You have to put gas in the car; it won't run without it. That little red light indicates how much gas you have—or, in your case, don't have. Some call it an 'idiot light,' and you obviously didn't notice it. There's nothing wrong with the car that some gasoline won't fix. Go get a refill!"

In many ways, marriage is a lot like that new car. Our marriages might be cruising along, but at some point they start to slow down and sputter. Too many people think, *Something's wrong with my ride. It's time to turn it in for a new model.* No, it's not. It's simply time to refill your tank. You need a refill as a husband; you need a refill as a wife. This is part of the commitment you made when you pledged to be husband and wife. The refill in this case isn't gasoline, but something a whole lot more powerful: the spiritual energy supplied by the Holy Spirit. "Be filled with the Spirit," God says to you.

The objective here is not to trade in your spouse for a new model but to turn your marriage into a classic, like the shining Duesenbergs and restored Packards that strut their stuff in slow-moving, classic-car parades. Give your marriage the regular, loving maintenance it needs to turn it into something that those around you can admire.

None of us can be the husband or the wife that God has called us to be without the help and filling of the Spirit. In our own strength, we will utterly fail. It is only as we are continually filled with and yielded to the Spirit that we can be a husband or wife in a thoroughly classic marriage.

Let's pray and ask God to fill us with His Spirit, to help us make a new commitment to strengthen our marriages. That is, after all, His desire.

+ MARRIAGE BUILDER

This is a command for all Christians. The present tense rules out any once-for-all reception of the Spirit but points to a continuous replenishment (literally, "go on being filled"). . . . There may, therefore, be successive fillings of the Spirit; indeed, the Christian life should be an uninterrupted filling. A. SKEVINGTON WOOD[1]

TiLL Death DO US Part

Therefore what God has joined together, let man not separate.
MATTHEW 19:6

I USED TO BE the proud owner of a 1957 Bel Air convertible. It had been beautifully restored and stood out from other cars because I kept it in good running condition. Besides, it looked just great (it didn't hurt that it was turquoise in color). When I would stop at a light, some guy would inevitably pull up next to me, with eyes wide, and ask what year the car was.

"1957," I'd tell him.

The good thing about cars of that era is that they were made of solid steel. When I'm rumbling down the road, I feel as if I am driving a tank! My Bel Air doesn't have all the new safety features of today's cars, but it's a classic. I wouldn't think of trading it in for a new Hyundai.

The truth is, it feels great when someone comes up to me and wistfully says, "Man, they don't make 'em like that anymore." Such comments make all the maintenance well worth the effort.

Not long ago, I was sitting in my '57 with my wife at a stoplight when some guy on a Harley pulled up alongside.

"I can't tell you how many of these '57s we used to put bullet holes in," he said.

Immediately I stiffened. *Is this guy thinking of using us for target practice?*

My anxiety quickly eased when he added, "You got a nice looking one," then roared off. He was just being friendly in a Harley kind of a way, I suppose. It seemed to be his way of saying that something he once regarded as junk could look beautiful today.

The same is true with our marriages—but we need to remember that they all require loving, regular maintenance. Every one of us can choose to turn our marriage into a classic—and you just don't get a classic by treating it like a clunker.

It's a wonderful thing when someone asks how long you've been married and you can give a number in double digits. When people ask me how long I have been married, I tell them, "Twenty-nine years."

"Really?" they say, looking at me. Then they look at Cathe and say, "No way! She just doesn't look old enough." (No one has yet to say that about me!)

Although being married for twenty-nine years is certainly rare in today's world, it doesn't have to be. God wants our marriages to last a lifetime, "till death do us part," as the wedding vows say.

Not only does He want our marriages to last, but He's also given us the manual on how to accomplish the feat, and He supplies us with all the power to make it happen. He has already freely given us every resource we need to build a classic marriage. All we need to do is use them. If we do, not even a pistol-packin' Harley rider can put so much as a dent in the marriage masterpiece we will build.

+   MARRIAGE BUILDER

If we deeply believe that the Lord is able to work on our behalf in all circumstances, then no collection of marital setbacks will prompt us to seriously consider divorce or withdrawal. If God is really as powerful as He claims to be, then the path of obedience will always lead to His intended purposes. The hope (better, the *certainty*) that God is at work to accomplish His plan even in the most difficult of marriages must remain firmly rooted in our awareness of His powerful grace—and that is Building Block 1. DR. LARRY CRABB[2]

The secret to Love

Jacob served seven years for Rachel, and they seemed only a few days to him because of the love he had for her. GENESIS 29:20 (NKJV)

THROUGHOUT MY YEARS AS a pastor, I have spoken with many couples who have just gotten to know each other yet want to rush into marriage. I like to remind them of the story of Jacob and Rachel. It's a classic love story. Jacob knew immediately that he wanted to marry Rachel, and he wasted no time in making his intentions known. After Jacob had spent a month with the family of his bride-to-be, his Uncle Laban said to him, "Just because you are a relative of mine, should you work for me for nothing? Tell me what your wages should be" (Genesis 29:15). Jacob didn't beat around the bush. He quickly replied, "I'll work for you seven years in return for your younger daughter Rachel" (v. 18).

Laban realized a good bargain when he saw one, so he replied, in essence, "Jacob, I will strike a deal with you. You work for me for seven years and you can have my daughter Rachel as your wife."

Jacob agreed, the seven years quickly passed, and at last the long-awaited wedding day arrived. Jacob no doubt felt enormous excitement as he was finally about to consummate his marriage with the beautiful Rachel. Imagine his surprise the next morning when he discovered that the woman lying next to him was actually Rachel's older sister, Leah! As Jacob's eyes adjusted to the morning light, he learned the awful truth. Somehow, Laban had tricked him into marrying the wrong woman. Outraged, Jacob stormed over to Laban and protested, "Why did you give me Leah? I worked seven years for *Rachel!*"

"We have a custom in our culture," Laban calmly explained, "that you always marry off the older daughter first. If you work for me seven more years, however, you can have Rachel, too."

Most men probably would have exploded at such a request and left town in a huff. Not Jacob. He worked seven more years. Do you know why? The secret is found in Genesis 29:20: "Jacob served seven years for Rachel, and they seemed *only a few days to him* because of the love he had for her" (NKJV, emphasis mine).

That is the kind of love that will last a lifetime—not merely love at first sight. What is so special about love at first sight, anyway? It is when two people have been looking at each other for years that love becomes special. I have been looking at my wife, Cathe, for twenty-nine years now, and she looks better all the time.

Jacob's initial infatuation gave way to a committed love—and that is the kind of love that husbands and wives need to cultivate for one another. Nothing else will do.

+ MARRIAGE BUILDER

> We need to view the wedding ceremony far more seriously than we have. When a man and woman stand before the minister, they are standing before God, and when they make their vows to each other, they are also making them to God, who will hold us accountable for what we promise. Based on that, we should commit that the word "divorce" will never be uttered with regard to our marriages, for divorce simply is not an option. AL JANSSEN[3]

radical love

Many waters cannot quench love; rivers cannot wash it away. If one were to give all the wealth of his house for love, it would be utterly scorned.
SONG OF SOLOMON 8:7

THE LOVE THAT GOD wants husbands and wives to express for each other is far more than a mere feeling of attachment. It is more than a romantic notion. Rather, it is a radical, life-changing, lifelong commitment that must be cultivated and nurtured.

Learning to love radically takes lots and lots of time. It does not happen overnight. I freely admit that initial attraction often brings a man and a woman together, but I also insist that such feelings won't necessarily last forever. If you count on initial "chemistry" to keep you going "till death do us part," you are due for some rough times.

Do you remember when you first fell in love? Maybe it was an elementary school crush. (I was constantly falling in love with girls who didn't even know I existed.) Do you remember when you first fell in love with your spouse? You probably felt great excitement and physical attraction as well as some bizarre symptoms—butterflies in the stomach, light-headedness, loss of appetite, paralysis of the tongue in the presence of your beloved. I've heard some people say they wanted this kind of love for a lifetime. Not me!

If your initial infatuation lasted forever, can you imagine the scene, even after twenty years of marriage? "Hi honey!" *I don't know what else to say to her. I'm just so nervous!* "What's for breakfast?" *I don't even have an appetite. Why am I even saying that?* "I didn't sleep all night. I have butterflies in my stomach." *I hope she doesn't notice my sweaty palms!*

Cathe would no doubt reply, "Greg, I think you're having a heart attack!"

We need to mature in our love. Do you remember the day you passed your first driving test? (I failed mine three times.) Remember how exciting it was? It felt as if you had sprouted wings. Now you could go where and when you wanted, so long as you had money for gas. You loved to climb behind the wheel and navigate your vehicle to some new destination. You would even look for excuses to drive.

Fast forward to today. Does driving a car continue to be such a thrill? Of course not. You can't expect to have that initial excitement for the rest of your life—and the same is true for marriage.

You can't build a solid, fulfilling marriage on the initial attraction that brought you together. You have to grow beyond the infatuation, learn that there is more to love than emotions. Real love, radical love, requires a life-long commitment—and only those who make such a commitment ever taste the extraordinary fruit that commitment alone produces.

+ MARRIAGE BUILDER

The state called "being in love" usually does not last. If the old fairy-tale ending "They lived happily ever after" is taken to mean "They felt for the next fifty years exactly as they felt the day before they were married," then it says what probably never was nor ever could be true, and would be highly undesirable if it were. Who could bear to live in that excitement for even five years? What would become of your work, your appetite, your sleep, your friendships? But, of course, ceasing to be "in love" need not mean ceasing to love. C. S. LEWIS[4]

active love

Love is patient, love is kind. It does not envy, it does not boast, it is not proud. It is not rude, it is not self-seeking, it is not easily angered, it keeps no record of wrongs. Love does not delight in evil but rejoices with the truth. It always protects, always trusts, always hopes, always perseveres.

1 CORINTHIANS 13:4-7

IN 1 CORINTHIANS 13, the apostle Paul shines the concept of love through a prism, revealing at least fifteen brilliant colors and hues. Each dazzling ray gives us a different facet of agape love to examine and embrace for ourselves. Yet this famous passage does not focus so much on what love *is,* but rather on what love *does* and *does not* do.

God's agape love—the unconditional love that husbands and wives are to express toward one another—is active. It is not abstract. It is not passive. It does not merely *feel* patient; it *is* patient. Agape love practices and delights in patience. It does not merely strive for feelings of kindness; rather, it does kind things.

Agape love means action, not merely a benign attitude. It means personal involvement, not just a comfortable detachment from the needs of others. Agape love means unconditionally loving the unlovable, reaching out to the undeserving, and serving the unresponsive. When we tap into God's agape love, we can love our mate even in the face of extremely unlovable behavior. Agape love is real only when it acts.

Look carefully at the Scripture passage at the top of this page. Do you see the magnificent portrait it paints? Every time you read the word *love,* substitute the name Jesus, and you're sure to see His marvelous profile. Jesus is patient and is kind. Jesus is not self-seeking. Jesus is not rude. Only one name fits perfectly in 1 Corinthians 13, and that is the name of Jesus Christ. In this passage, we see a beautiful picture of Jesus Himself—and also the model each of us is called to follow as we love our mate.

Insert your own name into the passage above. It may cause you to squirm a bit, but try it. John is patient. Mary is not rude. Jim is not self-seeking. Susan is not proud. I suggest this exercise, not to make you feel guilty, but to help you see where you might get a little more active in your expression of agape love toward your mate.

Whatever you do, don't sit on your hands and try to *feel* a certain way toward your husband or wife. Feelings are certainly important, but they make a better caboose than an engine. Get active—get up and do something loving for your spouse. The feelings you desire will eventually come rolling along behind.

✝   MARRIAGE BUILDER

When you love you wish to do things for. You wish to sacrifice for. You wish to serve. ERNEST HEMINGWAY[5]

pursuing kindness

Love is kind. 1 CORINTHIANS 13:4

YOU MIGHT TURN TO Shakespeare to be entertained, but don't trust the Bard for advice on marriage—at least not the well-known words from his *Taming of the Shrew:*

> *She shall watch all night,*
> *And if she chance to nod I'll rail and brawl,*
> *And with the clamour keep her still awake.*
> *This is a way to kill a wife with kindness.*[6]

Kindness it's not. Believe me, keeping your wife awake all night with loud noises will not earn you the description of "kind." If you want to see what kindness is all about, look to God. It is His kindness that won us over in the first place. As the apostle Paul reminds us, "God's kindness leads you toward repentance" (Romans 2:4). As you demonstrate God-powered kindness toward your spouse, your home will experience the same kind of peace and healing that your soul finds in repentance.

Make it your goal to express your love in practical acts of kindness. As corny as it may sound, thoughtful gifts like flowers or a gourmet meal still go a long way. Why not surprise your husband or wife with an unexpected little gift, something he or she isn't anticipating? If you come home with a present and say, "I want to tell you that I love you and I care about you," your act of kindness will do more than you could ever imagine to nurture your love for each other.

Consider the kindness of Jesus. During a long day of teaching and healing, He still fed the hungry multitudes. In the upper room, though He was keenly aware of His impending death on the cross, He humbly washed the dusty feet of His disciples, including those of the man He knew would soon betray Him. Even after His resurrection, Jesus took the time to fix breakfast for His famished followers.

Kindness is an active ingredient in agape love. Even something as simple as a kiss can go a long way. Did you know that researchers have discovered that kindness can actually lengthen your life? A group of German researchers (including psychologists, physicians, and insurance company representatives) cooperated on a project designed to find the secret to long life and success. They made a surprising discovery: a husband who kisses his wife each morning when he leaves for work lives longer!

In addition, the researchers found that men who kiss their wives have fewer automobile accidents on their way to work than men who omit the morning smooch. The good-morning kissers also miss less work because of sickness and earn 20 to 30 percent more than nonkissers do. Amazing!

So, husbands—when did you last kiss your wife and say, "I love you"?

Love is kind. Men, tell your wife that you love her today. Women, do the same for your husband. Give each other a kiss. Who knows? You might even live longer!

+   MARRIAGE BUILDER

One of the most difficult things to give away is kindness; it usually comes back to you. AUTHOR UNKNOWN

7

A second Honeymoon

Encourage one another and build each other up, just as in fact you are doing.
1 THESSALONIANS 5:11

YOUR WORDS HAVE A dramatic effect on your marriage. Proverbs 12:18 says, "Reckless words pierce like a sword, but the tongue of the wise brings healing." Scripture also says, "Death and life are in the power of the tongue, and those who love it will eat its fruit" (Proverbs 18:21, NKJV). That is why the Bible tells us that we should be "quick to listen, slow to speak and slow to become angry" (James 1:19). Agape love teaches us to build up and encourage our mates with positive words.

A woman wanted to divorce her husband and make him really suffer. So she went to a lawyer and told him, "I want to divorce my husband. I know that I am going to get control of most of his assets, but I want to make his life miserable. What could I do?"

"Have you told him yet?" the attorney asked. She hadn't. "Okay," he continued, "here's the plan. For three months, don't criticize him. Speak only well of him and build him up. Every time he does something right, commend him for it and tell him what a great guy he is. Do that for twelve weeks. When he thinks he has your full confidence and love—nail him! Tell him that you're filing for divorce. It will come as a complete shock!"

The woman loved the plan and was confident her husband would fall for it. For three months she complimented him, built him up, and said wonderful things to him. One day the lawyer called her back. "Are you ready to file?" he asked.

"Oh, no," the woman said. "We won't be needing your services. In fact, we're having a second honeymoon!" By taking a more positive tack and building up her husband, she actually helped to turn her marriage around.

Everyone can do what this woman did—including you. You can notice what your spouse has done right instead of only what he or she has done wrong. Weigh your words of complaint against your words of praise. Which side tips the balance? Your spouse craves praise and affirmation just as much as you do. Make it a point to say things like:

"Honey, I really appreciated it when you watched the kids today while I ran my errands."

"I am thankful that you are such a good provider for our family."

"I enjoyed our family time together this past weekend."

"You look really beautiful today."

Your mate needs to hear regular praise from you. Not only will it keep you far from the rocky shores of divorce, but it could also put you on your own blissful road to a second honeymoon.

+   MARRIAGE BUILDER

On your next date, ask each other about the primary way each of you feels love, expresses love. Then ask for opinions on how each of you perceives that the other expresses it and hears it. I'll guarantee an interesting conversation. And a valuable one. CAROLE MAYHALL[7]

Finding Fulfillment

He who finds a wife finds what is good and receives favor from the Lord.
PROVERBS 18:22

J. PAUL GETTY, ONE of the wealthiest men who ever lived, once said, "I would give my entire fortune for one happy marriage." Apparently he never found one.

A harmonious marriage is not only a great blessing spiritually, it is also good for us emotionally and physically. Countless studies have revealed that a strong and happy marriage causes both partners to live longer than those who are unmarried. They also need doctors and other health care services less often. Virtually every study of mortality and marital status shows that unmarried men and women have higher death rates, whether by accidents, disease, or self-inflicted wounds. Records dating back to the nineteenth century show that the highest suicide rates occur among the divorced, followed by the widowed and the never married. The lowest rates are among the married.

I heard the story of a young man who knew all about these statistics yet remained a bachelor throughout his twenties and thirties. When he was in his early thirties the church he served as a deacon began building a new facility, with members supplying much of the labor. As the building went up, the pastor invited all construction volunteers to write a favorite Bible verse on the interior beams before the workers installed the drywall. This young man chose a beam at the front of the new sanctuary and carefully scrawled out Proverbs 18:22: "He who finds a wife finds what is good and receives favor from the Lord." A little less than ten years later, he walked down the aisle with a beautiful young woman and today enjoys firsthand the many blessings of a God-centered marriage.

"I enjoyed life as a single," he said, "but I'm delighted to be married. In my bachelor days I used to get several colds a year, but in three years of marriage, I've had only one or two. This marriage thing really does agree with me!"

I propose to you that marriage can be the most fulfilling thing you will know in this life, next to your relationship with God. It can succeed beyond your dreams. It can flourish beyond your expectations. It can become something more than wonderful in your life, so long as you do it God's way.

And one more thing. If you're enjoying a happy marriage, you have something more than one of the wealthiest men who ever lived. Don't forget to thank God for that!

+ MARRIAGE BUILDER

Take each other for better or worse, but not for granted. ARLENE DAHL[8]

Be content

Like an apple tree among the trees of the forest is my lover among the young
men. I delight to sit in his shade, and his fruit is sweet to my taste.
SONG OF SOLOMON 2:3

THERE'S ALMOST NOTHING LIKE the sweetness of a crisp green apple, plucked just moments before from a towering tree that now offers cool shade from the late afternoon sun. That's contentment, and that's the lovely picture the Bible provides regarding marriage.

Have you ever thought of your marriage like that? As a source of rich, deep, sweet contentment? You'll find such satisfaction only when you release your unreasonable expectations and delight in what you have.

"As a teenager," writes Dale Hanson Bourke, "I imagined that I'd marry a man who brought me flowers regularly, called me 'darling,' and never failed to hold the door as I passed through it. I would prepare wonderful, candlelit dinners each night, would wear beautiful robes even on Saturday mornings, and would never, ever nag my husband. Fortunately, I gave up those dreams long before I had the chance to drive myself or Tom crazy with expectations neither of us could meet. It's not that we've forgotten the place of such nice touches in our marriage; it's just that they aren't the kinds of things that a marriage is built on."[9]

No one who believes the grass is always greener on the other side of the fence can find contentment. Think about when you were single. You probably said, "I'm so lonely. If only I were married, then I would be happy." But after your wedding, you may have thought, *I remember the good old days when I was single. I could go anywhere and do anything I wanted. Now I have all these responsibilities!* Married people often envy singles, and singles often envy those who are married. The fact is, there are advantages and disadvantages to both sets of circumstances.

God wants us to be content where we are right now. The apostle Paul writes, "I have learned in whatever state I am, to be content" (Philippians 4:11, NKJV). The writer of Hebrews adds, "Be content with such things as you have. For He Himself has said, 'I will never leave you nor forsake you' " (13:5, NKJV). The secret of contentment stems from our awareness of the Lord's constant presence in our lives—and the understanding that His presence is what we need most. Our contentment then spills over into every aspect of our lives.

I love the words of Psalm 37:4: "Delight yourself in the Lord and he will give you the desires of your heart." The word *delight* here means "to gladden or take joy in." God doesn't say, "Delight yourself in the Lord if He gives you the spouse of your dreams." Rather, He says simply to delight in Him. If we do that, He promises to give us the desires of our hearts. And what could provide more contentment than that?

+   M A R R I A G E   B U I L D E R

It is immature to think that the person I married thirty years ago, when she was eighteen, is the same person now at the age of forty-eight. It is unfair for me to hold her to some youthful expectation I may have had about our relationship. We both have made significant changes—physically, emotionally, spiritually, vocationally. We are different people. Life has developed us, shaped us, molded us . . . hopefully for the better. BILL CARMICHAEL[10]

vive La Différence!

This is now bone of my bones and flesh of my flesh; she shall be called "woman," for she was taken out of man. GENESIS 2:23

FOR QUITE SOME TIME, we've heard that men and women are really not so different from one another. In other words, men and women are essentially the same, except for the packaging. Some people say that everything we believed in the past regarding the contrast between the sexes is archaic and no longer acceptable.

But as anyone who has ever been married can attest, one fact is abundantly clear: men and women are *completely* different. Both scientific studies and our own observations support this truth. My wife and I, for example, are polar opposites when it comes to our television preferences.
I watch four programs at once; the commercials are my cue to move to the next program. My wife, on the other hand, might sit down to watch a cooking show from beginning to end. "Greg," she'll say, "come up and watch this show with me." Now, I really don't want to watch the cooking show, but I will do it just to be with her. (I do enjoy the new recipes she learns, too!)

Even the way we eat shows our differences. When Cathe and I go out to a restaurant, she often orders soup and/or salad. To me, salad is merely a warm-up for the real meal; it just helps make sure the jaw muscles are working and the taste buds are in gear. Soup is even more worthless. Still, I'll go to a soup and salad place with Cathe—and then sneak in a burger later.

My wife's latest passion is riding bikes. She will pedal for forty-five miles (or more) in one day. Lately she has been trying to get me into it. I borrowed a bike the other day, and while we were out riding in the sunshine, Cathe called back, "Isn't this wonderful? Just look at the birds and the clear blue sky. Don't you love it?"

"Yeah, I love it," I said, panting and pedaling. "But I prefer my other bike with the big engine—my Harley."

"This is better than the Harley," she declared.

"No it isn't," I wheezily replied. "When I'm on the Harley I still get to look at the birds and everything, but a hill's no problem. You just give it some gas and you're over it. But when you're on a bicycle and you see that same hill, you say, 'Oh no!' "

Men and women are different, and God intended things to be exactly that way. Even apart from the anatomical differences, a man is not a woman and a woman is not a man. So let's be thankful for that and join the French in exclaiming, "Vive la différence!"

+ MARRIAGE BUILDER

By creating a person *like* Adam yet very *unlike* Adam, God provided the possibility of a profound unity that otherwise would have been impossible. There is a different kind of unity enjoyed by the joining of diverse counterparts than is enjoyed by joining two things just alike. When we all sing the same melody line it is called unison, which means "one sound." But when we unite diverse lines of soprano and alto and tenor and bass, we call it harmony; and everyone who has an ear to hear knows that something deeper in us is touched by great harmony than by mere unison. So God made a woman and not another man. He created heterosexuality, not homosexuality. JOHN PIPER[11]

something's missing

The Lord God said, "It is not good for the man to be alone. I will make a helper suitable for him." GENESIS 2:18

HE ENJOYED THE ULTIMATE bachelor's life: an all-expense-paid, roomy apartment with a fabulous view; a pantry fully stocked with all his favorite foods; a job that he loved and that gave him tremendous fulfillment; a flexible schedule of his own choosing; the freedom to travel; and a total absence of threats to his safety or opposition to his lifestyle.

And yet something was missing. Even God said so.

You will recall that God created Adam in His own image and placed him in a veritable paradise known as the Garden of Eden. Adam had the ultimate job description. He was to discover the secrets of the garden that God had made and then walk in harmony and fellowship with his Creator. The Lord would even show up at an appointed time each afternoon to spend time with Adam (see Genesis 3:8). Life was grand. Adam lived in an unspoiled paradise, with the entire animal kingdom to bring him a sense of companionship.

Still, something wasn't quite right. Adam didn't know what it was, because that something did not yet exist. But God knew.

"The Lord God said, 'It is not good for the man to be alone. I will make a helper suitable for him.' . . . The man said, " 'This is now bone of my bones and flesh of my flesh; she shall be called "woman," for she was taken out of man'" (Genesis 2:18, 23).

This is the first time in the biblical narrative that God calls something in Eden "not good." As surely as God had created Adam with a void in his life for Him, He also created him with a need for another person. So God made Eve and brought her to the man.

In the original Hebrew, the word *helper* means "someone who assists another to reach fulfillment." It is used elsewhere in the Old Testament to describe someone who comes to the rescue of another. And Adam needed this "helper." God designed Eve to provide what was missing in Adam's life. God sent the woman to rescue the man from loneliness, and vice versa. As Ecclesiastes 4:9-10 says, "Two are better than one, because they have a good return for their work: If one falls down, his friend can help him up. But pity the man who falls and has no one to help him up!"

Adam had a good life before the woman was made, but it couldn't hold a candle to his situation after God sent Eve into his world. She was just what the doctor ordered, so to speak.

She still is.

+   MARRIAGE BUILDER

It is the glory of woman that she is more responsive than man to what is around her. That is what makes life beautiful. How dull and cold and barbarous life would be if only cold-blooded men were here to confront the world of creation! Women add that quality of tenderness, softness, empathy, sympathy, and comfort to the world. They add something that no man can give. RAY STEDMAN[12]

Adam's Rib

The man gave names to all the livestock, the birds of the air and all the beasts of the field. But for Adam no suitable helper was found. So the Lord God caused the man to fall into a deep sleep; and while he was sleeping, he took one of the man's ribs and closed up the place with flesh. Then the Lord God made a woman from the rib he had taken out of the man, and he brought her to the man. GENESIS 2:20-22

THE PATIENT PROCLAIMED THE first surgery in history a total success. "This is now bone of my bones and flesh of my flesh," cried Adam upon getting his first look at Eve, fresh from God's operating room. "She shall be called 'woman,' for she was taken out of man" (Genesis 2:23).

Adam immediately recognized that Eve was his special companion and life partner—and he could not have felt any more delighted. He sensed that here was someone who could help him reach personal fulfillment and maximum satisfaction. His life in the garden was already idyllic—but now it could reach even greater heights.

Commentator Matthew Henry said of Eve, "If man is the head, she is the crown, a crown to her husband, the crown of the visible creation. The man was dust refined, but the woman was dust double-refined, one remove further from the earth."

The moment he saw Eve, Adam knew he had been given a treasure beyond anything he'd ever known. He exulted in this greatest blessing from God. Although he might be missing a rib, he had gained the love of his life.

On a side note, I once heard about a conversation between Adam and Eve not recorded in Scripture. One night, when Adam came home late, Eve was upset and the two began arguing.

"Where have you been?" she said. "Have you been seeing other women?"

"Are you crazy?" Adam replied. "You are the only woman on the face of the earth!"

The next morning, Adam woke up to find Eve poking at his side.

"What are you doing?" he asked, perplexed.

Eve looked up and said, "Just counting your ribs."

Seriously, have you considered how unique it is that God would choose to make woman out of the rib of man? Here's Matthew Henry's perspective: "The woman was made of a rib out of the side of Adam; not made out of his head to rule over him, nor out of his feet to be trampled upon by him, but out of his side to be equal with him, under his arm to be protected, and near his heart to be beloved."

Equal, protected, and beloved. Just what every Eve longs for!

+ MARRIAGE BUILDER

It takes great maturity to be selfless. Only a mature individual can put the needs of another over his own needs. It takes a mature man to be polite, to use encouraging words, and to keep a positive attitude in the face of strong opposition. But a mature man of God is marked by his love. PHIL DOWNER[13]

your Best Friend

The Lord has been witness between you and the wife of your youth; ... She is your companion and your wife by covenant. MALACHI 2:14 (NKJV)

WHAT COMES TO MIND when you think of a best friend? When I looked up "best friend" on the Web, I discovered that canines were the most popular response. I found "My Best Friend—great gifts for the dog lover!" as well as dog.com, alleydog.com, bestfriends.com, Man's Best Friend Software, The Dog's Best Friend, Best Friend Pet Adoption, and many others.

Now, I have nothing against Fido, but I have to say that if he's your best friend—in place of your spouse—then you're probably headed for trouble. Certainly there's a place for Rex or Lassie, but I believe your best friend really should be your wife or your husband. When people ask me, "Who is your best friend?" and I tell them it's my wife, they often don't believe me. But she *is* my best friend!

When I have a day off, I want to spend it with her. When I face a conflict, I want to discuss it with her and seek her godly input. Sometimes we just sit and read together, without speaking so much as a word. The point is, I *want* to be with her.

Does that mean I lack friendships outside of my marriage or that I don't take time to be with others? Of course not. But it does mean that I have a greater commitment to Cathe than to anyone else because she is my "help meet"—to use the old King James vernacular—my companion in life.

God wants husbands and wives to become really close friends. Malachi 2:14 (NKJV) tells us, "The Lord has been witness between you and the wife of your youth, with whom you have dealt treacherously; yet she is your companion and your wife by covenant." A man's wife is to be his companion. The word *companion* means "one with whom you are united in thoughts, goals, plans, and efforts." To describe the same thing today, we'd probably use the term *best friend.*

Take a look at your marriage. Are you united with your spouse in thoughts, goals, plans, and efforts? Do you look forward to spending time alone together, just "hanging out"? Do you consider your mate a good friend, even your best friend? If you want a satisfying marriage, that's a worthy goal to work toward.

I doubt that ten-year-old Kirsten, quoted on a marriage Web site, grew up in a "best friends" kind of home. When asked, "How do you decide whom to marry?" she replied, "No person really decides before they grow up who they're going to marry. God decides it all way before, and you get to find out later who you're stuck with."

You needn't "get stuck" with anybody. Work toward making your spouse your best friend, and watch your satisfaction grow.

+ MARRIAGE BUILDER

I missed [my wife] on Mother's Day. The covenant between us is very deep. One of the boys was writing something for her. He came to me and asked, "Is there a verse about moms?" I said, "Yes. Why don't you use this one: 'Her children rise up and call her blessed; her husband also, and he praises her' " [Proverbs 31:28, NKJV]. JOHN PIPER[14]

The Need to Leave

For this reason a man will leave his father and mother.   GENESIS 2:24

YOU CAN'T REALLY START some things without leaving something else behind.

You can't start walking without leaving behind your attachment to crawling.

You can't start riding a bike without leaving behind your fear of falling.

Likewise, you can't successfully start a marriage without first leaving behind your dependence on Mom and Dad. Biblically, marriage begins with a man leaving his father and mother—as well as all other relationships. Notice that God specifies leaving behind the closest relationship we have outside of marriage, thus implying that all lesser ties must also be broken, changed, or left behind.

To show just how strongly He feels about this "leaving," God repeats this command several times throughout Scripture. Jesus quotes Genesis 2:24 in His own instruction on marriage (Matthew 19:5; Mark 10:7), and the apostle Paul adds his voice to the chorus in Ephesians 5:31. These multiple declarations suggest that someone who cannot "leave" is simply not ready for marriage.

Why does God give such an instruction? Because the man's primary commitment must be to his wife, and the wife's primary commitment must be to her husband. The new husband and wife are to continue to honor their parents, but a definite leaving must take place.

Some men and women struggle with this idea; they find it hard to break free from Mom and Dad. Because they crave their parents' approval in everything they do, at the first marital disagreement, they "run home to Mommy," so to speak.

I once heard a story about some newlyweds who moved far away from home and into an apartment building. The wife struck up a friendship with an elderly woman who lived upstairs, and the neighbor soon became a sort of second mother. One evening, the young couple had a terrible fight and the new bride fled upstairs to her friend's apartment. She poured out her heart and asked to stay the night. "I'm sorry, dear," the woman replied, "but no." And with that she closed her door. With nowhere else to go, the stunned young woman returned to her own apartment—and she and her husband quickly patched up their disagreement.

That wise and kind older woman understood the necessity of leaving—and because of her commitment to God's instruction, the young couple "made it."

Please understand that in no way do I want to diminish the important influence or advice that godly parents can provide. Nevertheless, I maintain that a husband and wife—having formed a new union—must learn how to resolve their own conflicts. They need to realize that a new union, a new family, has emerged. And the first thing they must do, according to God's Word, is "leave" the households of their youth.

✣   MARRIAGE BUILDER

It's clear that a boy must leave his parents in order to become a man. As we just read, "a man shall leave." If a boy decides to pursue manhood, he will leave. But Genesis 2:24 gives us something else interesting. It says that the reason for leaving is the woman of Genesis 2:23. This means that there is a sense in which the woman plays a big role in helping the boy become a man. She motivates him to leave. DAVID DEWITT[15]

sticking together
or just plain stuck?

For this cause a man shall leave his father and his mother, and shall cleave to his wife; and they shall become one flesh. GENESIS 2:24 (NASB)

A GOOD START IS certainly better than a bad one, but we must remember that a start is nothing more than that: a start. If we don't pay careful attention to what comes next, the best start in the world does us little good. The same is true in marriage. Although all good marriages start with a "leaving," they must quickly lead to something else in order to capitalize on their excellent beginning. Biblically, that next step is "cleaving," a concept that might require some explanation.

When we hear the English word *cleave,* we usually think of severing something, like a meat cleaver does. The word in Hebrew, however, means just the opposite—"to adhere to, to stick, or to be attached with some strong tie."

To cleave effectively requires determined action. We might compare it to mountain climbing. When you climb a mountain, you are not "stuck" to it, but you hang on to the face of the big rock and dig in. Why? Because you value your life and you want to be around tomorrow. So you hang on and keep climbing; you determinedly "cleave" to the mountain.

Marriage is the same way. We are not simply "stuck" together, but with determination and strength we hold on to and adhere to one another. There is nothing passive about the act of cleaving!

In the New Testament, the Greek word translated *cleave* means "to cement together; to stick like glue so the two will be welded together and cannot be separated without serious damage to both."

Have you ever tried to break apart something that has been welded together? Or have you ever fooled around with superglue? I have. I've used that remarkable adhesive to assemble various models—and I am the messiest "gluer" on the planet. Inevitably I do the one thing the manufacturer says not to do: I wind up with my thumb and forefinger cemented together. They *cleave* to one another like nobody's business.

A husband and a wife need to cleave to each other like superglued fingers. Of course, when the Bible says that a man and woman become "one flesh," it is speaking in far more than metaphorical terms. Something extraordinary happens within the bond of marriage that makes two persons one. "So then," Jesus says, "they are no longer two but one flesh. Therefore what God has joined together, let not man separate" (Matthew 19:6, NKJV).

Because this "one flesh" relationship is wonderfully true, we should periodically take stock of our marriages and ask, "Is there any relationship or pursuit of mine that could potentially put distance between me and my mate? Is it building up my marriage or tearing it down? Am I cleaving to my spouse?"

If you want to climb the marriage mountain and reach the summit safely, you have no option but to cleave.

+   MARRIAGE BUILDER

What will you do . . . when unexpected tornadoes blow through your home, or when the doldrums leave your sails sagging and silent? Will you pack it in and go home to Mama? Will you pout and cry and seek ways to strike back? Or will your commitment hold you steady? These questions must be addressed now, before Satan has an opportunity to put his noose of discouragement around your neck. Set your jaw and clench your fists. Nothing short of death must ever be permitted to come between the two of you. Nothing! DR. JAMES DOBSON[16]

the secret to marriage

A woman is bound to her husband as long as he lives. 1 CORINTHIANS 7:39

PEOPLE HAVE OFTEN ASKED me to reveal the secret to a successful marriage. In my case, the answer is that I married Cathe. But since *you* can't do that, let's consider a bedrock principle that everyone can apply to his or her own marital relationship.

When Cathe and I got married, we heeded the advice of Benjamin Franklin, who once said, "Keep your eyes wide open before and half shut afterwards." A lot of folks who run into problems in their marriage do the opposite. They half shut their eyes before they get married and open them wide right after.

Cathe and I took our time. We courted for three years. We endured big, dramatic breakups that seemed to become annual events—the type of break-ups where we said, "I never want to see your face again. It is over with!" But it wasn't over with, because whether we knew it or not, in our hearts we had already committed ourselves to one another.

And that's the secret: commitment.

Naturally, as Cathe and I spent time apart, our love only grew. Eventually I began to realize that she was the only girl for me. And more than a quarter of a century later, we're still a happy couple.

I can remember our wedding day as though it happened yesterday. A vision of beauty, walking gracefully down the aisle, took my breath away. I, on the other hand, looked like mountain man Jeremiah Johnson, just in from the woods. I had a bushy red beard and long hair reaching to my shoulders and parted in the middle. Underneath all that hair, however, my wife could see that there was a . . . bald man in the making! Nevertheless, on that wonderful day, we made our commitment to each other both official and public.

Wedlock should be a padlock. Getting married should be as permanent and secure as turning a lock and throwing away the key. Marriage means standing by the commitment we have made, come what may.

Such an attitude prompts me to think of an astute comment made by Winston Churchill during World War II. "Victory," he said, "is not won through evacuation." He held his ground even when the Nazis began bombing London day and night. Inspired by their leader's courage, the British people simply would not give up.

We need that same attitude in marriage. Sure, the bombs will drop. Of course the problems will come. But despite the inevitable struggles, we need to say, "We are going to make it. We are not evacuating. We are going to stick this out. And we will prevail."

Marriage is all about commitment. And there is no secret greater than that.

+ MARRIAGE BUILDER

> If our confidence in God's grace is sufficient to maintain hope when despair seems justified, then we are in a position to commit ourselves to doing whatever God says. We can act on the strength of our hope by persisting to work on our marriages even when tempted to quit. DR. LARRY CRABB[17]

god's good will for you

You need to persevere so that when you have done the will of God, you will receive what he has promised. HEBREWS 10:36

BEFORE WE'RE MARRIED, MOST of us do a lot of wondering about whether this girlfriend or that boyfriend might turn out to be "God's will" for us—that is, whether we might be dating our future spouse.

My friend's wife has a story right in line with this. For their second or third date, my friend invited this young woman and her roommate to his house for a home-cooked lasagna dinner. She says that as she watched him sitting in his favorite chair, choosing some background music for their meal, she suddenly thought, *Am I looking at my future husband?* Over the next several months of dating, she pondered that question more rigorously. *Could it be God's will for me to marry this man?*

Once she decided that the answer was "yes," she also said yes to his proposal of marriage. And now they're both enjoying God's will for their lives. For them, the question of "Is this the right one?" has been settled forever—regardless of the problems they may yet have to face.

Have you ever considered that once you say, "I do," you have unfailingly discovered God's will for your life in the area of marriage? After the vows have been said, you needn't spend a single second wondering whether your spouse is really God's will for you; in that moment, he or she has *become* God's will for you.

How could God make His will any more plain? "I hate divorce," He says in Malachi 2:16. "So guard yourself in your spirit, and do not break faith." Instead of spending any time wondering whether we might have made a mistake in choosing our husband or wife, God wants us to work to make His will for our lives feel what it actually is—namely, "good, pleasing, and perfect" (Romans 12:2).

I must tell you I feel great joy that God did not answer all of my prayers regarding "the right one" for me! The other day I saw a woman whom I had really liked when I was a teenager. At the time, I even thought she was "God's will" for me. But God said "no."

Back then, I groused about God's answer. But, ah, the clarity of 20/20 hindsight! As I observed this woman to whom the years had not been kind, then turned to look at my wife, all I could say was, "God knew what He was doing! His will is perfect!"

Those of us who are married have the privilege of living out God's perfect will for our married lives. His will for us, right now, is that we work hard to make our marriages the best they can be—even "good, pleasing, and perfect."

+ MARRIAGE BUILDER

> From the day you make that commitment [to say "I do"], your question about "the right person" is answered. He or she is the right person for you to stick to, love, cherish. He or she may not prove to be the right person to make you happy, but he or she is certainly the right person to shape you—in better or worse conditions, in sickness or in health, in poverty or in wealth—into the person God wants you to become. TIM STAFFORD[18]

Equal standing, Different Functions

I want you to know that the head of every man is Christ, the head of woman is man, and the head of Christ is God. 1 CORINTHIANS 11:3 (NKJV)

NO DIFFERENCE EXISTS BETWEEN men and women in their basic standing before God. Still, we cannot afford to miss an important principle of family authority expressed in the New Testament. The apostle Paul explains that man is the head of woman and Christ is the head of man, just as God is the head of Christ.

Before anyone objects to Paul's teaching, let's first try to understand his phrase, "the head of Christ is God." What exactly does he mean?

The Bible reveals to us a holy Trinity: the Father, the Son, and the Holy Spirit. These three persons constitute not three gods, but one God. Each member of the Trinity is fully God. The Son is just as much God as is the Father, and the Holy Spirit is just as much God as is the Son. Together they comprise the single, triune God. Nevertheless, although they remain eternally coequal, the Bible teaches that God the Father is the head of God the Son—not in essence or in nature, but in role or function.

Jesus—whom Isaiah called "Mighty God" (Isaiah 9:6)—laid aside many of the privileges of deity and took upon Himself the form of a servant, becoming obedient to death, even the death of the cross (see Philippians 2:8). When Jesus walked this earth, He repeatedly demonstrated His subservience to His Father. He spoke the words of the Father. He submitted to the wishes of the Father. Though He was "in the form of God" (Philippians 2:6, NKJV), though "it pleased the Father that in Him all the fullness should dwell" (Colossians 1:19, NKJV), and though Jesus is "the brightness of [God's] glory and the express image of His person" (Hebrews 1:3, NKJV), He willingly placed Himself in an obedient position.

In the same way, though the husband and the wife remain equal in their standing before God, in order for the family to function harmoniously, the woman—with no loss of dignity—is to willingly submit to the headship of her husband. To quote a statement of faith published by the Southern Baptist Convention, "The husband and wife are of equal worth before God, since both are created in God's image. The marriage relationship models the way God relates to His people. A husband is to love his wife as Christ loved the church. He has the God-given responsibility to provide for, to protect, and to lead his family. A wife is to submit graciously to the servant leadership of her husband even as the church willingly submits to the headship of Christ."[19]

Well said—and you know what else? It works! God intends that a wife's respect, help, and cooperation be matched by her husband's servant leadership as together they submit to the Lord Jesus Christ and to one another.

+   MARRIAGE BUILDER

When a man and woman perform a ballet and the man takes the lead and gives the cues, it never enters anyone's mind that by virtue of this he is a better dancer. On the contrary, her talent is magnified in the poised responsiveness and perfect adaptation that create a moment of art so harmonious that no one thinks about who is leading and who is following, but all simply admire the beautiful unity that the two have become. A marriage ought to be such a union—a work of art composed by the interweaving of maleness and femaleness. JOHN PIPER[20]

19

in and under authority

David said to Abigail, "Praise be to the Lord, the God of Israel, who has sent you today to meet me. May you be blessed for your good judgment and for keeping me from bloodshed this day and from avenging myself with my own hands." 1 SAMUEL 25:32-33

AS THE HEAD OF my home, I am a man in authority. As a follower of Christ, I am also a man under authority. As such, I have a spiritual responsibility to make the best decisions possible for my home, which means getting the best counsel I can—and that more often than not comes from my wife.

I think any man who understands godly leadership will greatly value what his wife has to say. God has placed me in authority as the head of my home, but that doesn't mean I stand around barking orders to Cathe. I recognize that she is an equal partner in this marriage, and therefore I seek her input. I urgently want to know her opinion.

I can think of multiple situations where I have been following a certain course, but after I've talked with my wife and heard her point of view, I will say, "Hmmm. I don't think I should go this way after all." I do not find it necessary in most cases to say, "Look, wife—I am the man! I am God's appointed leader, so we will go with my decision!" The majority of the time, Cathe and I will work out a solution and move forward together, and any husband who knows anything about life will do the same. I know David was glad that he listened to the counsel of Abigail—and that was *before* they were married!

We find the story in 1 Samuel 25. When a stubborn and surly man named Nabal (even his name means "foolish") deeply offended David and his men, David determined to wipe out the man's household. When Abigail, Nabal's intelligent and beautiful wife, discovered what her arrogant husband had done, she sought out David with gifts and persuaded him to avoid revenge. David, astonished by the woman's wisdom, exclaimed, "Praise be to the Lord, the God of Israel, who has sent you today to meet me. May you be blessed for your good judgment and for keeping me from blood-shed this day and from avenging myself with my own hands." Later, when Nabal died (of fright!), David himself married the man's remarkable widow.

Now, what would have happened had David ignored the advice of this most capable woman? For one thing, biblical history might well have been a great deal poorer than it is. If David had carried out his rash act, he might have disqualified himself from the lofty position God intended for him.

Of course, not every wife is an Abigail—but I also know there are too many Nabals who don't appreciate the wisdom and insight that God has imparted to their wives. Wise husbands let their Abigails shine!

+ MARRIAGE BUILDER

> A man who fears the Lord not only expects His Savior to hear and act on his cries for help, but he also follows his Savior's example. He, too, is attentive to the cries of his loved ones. He listens to them because God listens to him. A Christlike man strives to become like the Master, who was a master listener. FLOYD MCCLUNG, JR.[21]

just Love Her

Husbands, love your wives. EPHESIANS 5:25

THE BIBLE GIVES EVERY Christian husband a revolutionary three-word phrase that has the power to radically change any marriage: Love your wife. Four times in Ephesians 5:25-33, the apostle Paul instructs men to love their wives.

We husbands tend to gloss over this command, believing that we're already complying with God's instruction—but I think if we were to think through and apply this single commandment systematically, it would transform our marriages.

"But Greg," someone might say, "what about *her?* Isn't she supposed to submit?"

Yes, but you're missing the point. Don't even concern yourself with that issue. You focus on what God has called *you* to do. And if you will do your part, in most cases your wife will do hers. If you will begin to really love your wife, most likely she will respond in kind.

Does that sound implausible? Then think of it this way. Why are you a Christian in the first place? Why is it that you put your faith in Jesus? Probably it is because God loved you *unconditionally.* He accepted you as you were—in your ugly, helpless, sinful state—and began to transform and change you. It was His love that ultimately wore down your rebellion and resistance. The Bible says, "We love Him because He first loved us" (1 John 4:19, NKJV).

Our submission to Christ today is a direct result of His love toward us. We have come to see that His plans for us are good. We have come to see that even if God tells us to do something we don't like, it is always for our benefit. So we surrender to Him. It is difficult at times, but we do it. His love continually wins us over.

The same will be true in a marriage. If a wife can feel confident that her husband has her best interests at heart; if she can see that he loves her so deeply that he continually demonstrates an intense concern for her welfare—then it will be far easier for her to submit to his leadership.

A despairing man once called a friend because his wife was threatening to divorce him. With resignation in his voice, the dejected man asked his friend to pray for him. His friend said he would, but added, "The request I'm going to make in my prayers is that you stop being so acquiescent and fatalistic about all this. I know Mary and I know you. You two have had a good marriage—up to now. And a good marriage is worth fighting for." The man's friend then described love as presented in Henry Drummond's classic book *The Greatest Thing in the World*—inspired by 1 Corinthians 13—and challenged him to live out that kind of love. The man accepted his friend's challenge and ultimately saved his marriage.

Love has that kind of astonishing power. Try it for yourself, and enjoy the results.

+ MARRIAGE BUILDER

The call to love is not so much a call to a certain state of feeling as it is to a quality of action. When Paul says, "Love your wives," he is saying, "Be loving toward your wife—treat her as lovely." Do the things that are truly loving things. . . . How are husbands to love their wives? How much love is required of the man? Paul says like Christ loves the Church. R. C. SPROUL[22]

As christ Loved the church

Husbands, love your wives, just as Christ loved the church. EPHESIANS 5:25

HUSBAND, DO YOU WANT your marriage to grow strong? Then love your wife *as Christ loved the church.* Do you want your children to grow up walking with God? Then love your wife *as Christ loved the church.* Do you want your church to be a powerful witness in your community? Then love your wife *as Christ loved the church.* Do you want to help see our country enjoy a mighty spiritual awakening? Then love your wife *as Christ loved the church.*

This is a bedrock principle, a foundational truth that we absolutely must build into our marriages. When we husbands really begin to love our wives as Christ loved the church, it's like a spark that sets off a healing wildfire.

Notice, this is not any old kind of love. It's a special, others-centered, passionate kind of determined love that drives the lover to extraordinary lengths to bless the beloved. Consider just a few ways in which Christ loved His church:

- He gave up for a time the glories and comforts of heaven in order to become human, that He might identify with our weaknesses and temptations.
- He—the Lord of glory, the Lion of the tribe of Judah, the King of kings and Lord of lords—submitted to the authority of His human parents and remained obedient to their wishes while living under their roof.

- He stooped low to serve His disciples, showing them by personal example that the way to the top is found only on the road of humility.
- He who at any time could have commanded twelve legions of angels to end His cruel torture instead allowed Himself to be insulted, beaten, and crucified so that we might obtain eternal life through His willing sacrifice.

Does that help to clarify what Paul means when he tells husbands to love their wives "as Christ loved the church"? Although we can't give up the glories of heaven (because we haven't even been there yet), we can look for ways to willingly put ourselves out in order to lift up our wives. We can humbly serve our wives, refuse to demand our "rights," and joyfully seek to serve instead. That's a lot, I know. But the kind of love that Jesus Christ poured out for the church is exactly the kind of self-giving love that God wants us husbands to show our wives. Such a love may cost a lot, guys, but it buys more than we can imagine.

+   MARRIAGE BUILDER

Love as distinct from "being in love" is not merely a feeling. It is a deep unity, maintained by the will and deliberately strengthened by habit; reinforced by (in Christian marriages) the grace which both partners ask, and receive, from God. They can have this love for each other even at those moments when they do not like each other; as you love yourself even when you do not like yourself. They can retain this love even when each would easily, if they allowed themselves, be "in love" with someone else. "Being in love" first moved them to promise fidelity: this quieter love enables them to keep the promise. It is on this love that the engine of marriage is run: being in love was the explosion that started it. C. S. LEWIS[23]

sacrificiaL Love

Husbands, love your wives, just as Christ loved the church and gave himself up for her. EPHESIANS 5:25

HOW DID CHRIST LOVE the church? He loved His bride *sacrificially.* He gave up His own life that she might live. He shed His own blood that she might be cleansed of the stain of sin. He bound Himself that she might go free. In short, He sacrificed Himself, once for all, that she might experience the limitless delights of heaven, for all eternity.

In the same way, husbands are to nurture this kind of sacrificial love for their wives. And what is the motive for exhibiting such a love? Because she deserves it? Perhaps. But ultimately, we are to love like this simply because God has commanded it—and, as in everything, He led the way.

Did the church merit God's love when Jesus extended that love to her? Hardly. Scripture says, "But God demonstrates his own love for us in this: *While we were still sinners,* Christ died for us" (Romans 5:8, italics mine).

Did you, husband, immediately respond to the nudging of the Holy Spirit when He first brought you to a sense of your need for Jesus? Did you immediately believe in Christ the moment you heard the gospel message? Probably not. Most likely, you put it off for weeks, months, maybe even decades. But did God give up on you? Did He write you off and say, "Forget about it, loser"?

No. He kept on loving you. He kept calling you, month after month and year after year. And one day, you finally came to your senses and responded.

In the same sacrificial way, we husbands are to love our wives. God calls us to keep on loving her—day in and day out, month in and month out, year in and year out—just as Christ loved the church. Regardless of who she is or what she does.

In fact, the husband who loves his wife as Christ loved the church will give everything he has for her—even his life, if necessary. So if a loving husband is ready to sacrifice his life for his wife, then certainly he will eagerly make lesser sacrifices for her. That means putting his own likes, desires, preferences, and welfare aside. He will do whatever it takes to please her and meet her needs. He will die to self in order to love his wife.

Does the Bible give Christian husbands a radical model of masculinity? You bet. It takes a real man to sacrifice, to lay down his life and love his wife in such a self-giving manner. But a curious thing happens when the love of Christ compels us (see 2 Corinthians 5:14)—our sacrifice becomes less of a duty and more of a pleasure. And at that point, we begin to understand why Jesus endured the cross "for the joy set before him" (Hebrews 12:2).

+   MARRIAGE BUILDER

When the time came, the decision was firm. It took no great calculation. It was a matter of integrity. Had I not promised, forty-two years before, "in sickness and in health . . . till death do us part"? This was no grim duty to which I was stoically resigned, however, it was only fair. [My wife] had, after all, cared for me for almost four decades with marvelous devotion; now it was my turn. And such a partner she was! If I took care of her for forty years, I would never be out of her debt. ROBERTSON MCQUILKIN[24]

purifying love

Husbands, love your wives just as Christ also loved the church and gave Himself for her, that He might sanctify and cleanse her with the washing of water by the word, that He might present her to Himself a glorious church, not having spot or wrinkle or any such thing, but that she should be holy and without blemish. So husbands ought to love their own wives as their own bodies; he who loves his wife loves himself. EPHESIANS 5:25-28 (NKJV)

THE NUMBER ONE PRIORITY of all Christian husbands ought to be the spiritual lives of their families. God is one day going to hold us accountable for how effective we were as spiritual leaders. That is the high calling He has placed on our lives. We husbands are to exhibit a *purifying* love.

I believe that most men really do care for their families. I think that most husbands would lay down their very lives for their families if it came to that. Most men, if they were down to their last meal, would give it to their wife and kids.

We may not be facing physical threats or starvation, but we need to realize that we are facing a spiritual attack. An evil adversary named Satan wants to destroy our wives and children. Whereas I'm sure that most of us would rise to the challenge to defend our families physically, many of us do far too little when it comes to defending the spiritual front. We lack vigilance. We remain only half alert. A purifying love must remain fully alert and refuse to allow corrupting influences to creep in unobserved and unchallenged.

Husbands, we need to be the ones leading in spiritual matters. We should be the ones saying, "Let's pray together. Let's get in the Word. Let's go to church." We need to be the ones leading the way; that's what purifying love does.

May I ask—are you doing that? Are you the spiritual leader of your home? If you want to exhibit the purifying love to which God has called you, taking up the mantle of leadership is a necessary first step.

If only we would do our part, I believe that dramatic and startling results would follow. If we were really to begin shouldering the spiritual leadership of our homes, I think that we would soon notice incredible differences in our families. Purifying love dramatically changes for the better all that it touches.

Husbands, I urge you to take on this exciting, life-changing exercise as a challenge. And rest assured that God *will* give you the strength to do what He has called you to do. After all, He has a vested interest in helping you to become more like His Son!

+   MARRIAGE BUILDER

Marriage is a symbol for the love Christ gives his church. It is a sacrament, a means by which God conveys to the world his intention of how individuals are to love each other, how society is meant to love, how the members of the kingdom of God in heaven are even now loving each other. And that spiritual love is what has sustained our relationship; it is the rock at the very core of this marriage which has lasted despite everything. KAREN MAINS[25]

DweLL with understanding

Husbands, likewise, dwell with them with understanding, giving honor to the
wife, as to the weaker vessel, and as being heirs together of the grace of life,
that your prayers may not be hindered. 1 PETER 3:7 (NKJV)

THERE'S A LOT TO be said for knowing someone extremely well—
especially if that someone is your wife.

The term translated *dwell* in this verse does not mean merely to live
with one's wife; it means "to be aligned with" her. In other words, the apostle
here tells us that every Christian husband needs to know his wife's
strengths, weaknesses, hopes, aspirations, and fears. And such intimate
knowledge comes only through frequent conversation, careful listening,
and diligent observation.

One woman told writer Nathaniel Branden, "My husband has always
been my best audience. Whether it's something I did at work that day, or a
clever remark I made at a party, or the way I dress, or a meal I've prepared—
he seems to notice everything. He lets me see his pride and delight. I feel like
I'm standing in the most marvelous spotlight. I only hope I'm as good at
expressing my appreciation of him, because I'll tell you something: being
loved is the second-best thing in the world; loving someone is the best."[26]

This woman, whether she knows it or not, has anticipated Peter's next
instruction to Christian husbands. Not only are we to gain a deep understanding of our wives, but we are to use that knowledge to "honor" them. Do
you think this woman felt honored? Of course she did; that's why it felt as if

she stood "in the most marvelous spotlight." And did you notice her natural response? She aimed to do for her husband what he did for her, and match his appreciation for her with an equal appreciation of her own. And so begins the most delightful competition in the world.

Husband, what does your wife need right now? Do you know the problems or struggles she faces? What are her dreams? Just how well do you know your wife? And how are you using your knowledge to honor her?

If you're not honoring your wife, Peter has a word of warning for you. The apostle declares that failure to honor our wives by dwelling with them in an understanding way puts up a big roadblock to answered prayer. It's as if God has said, "The way you treat your wife is so important to me that I'm linking it to your prayer life. You may spend all day in prayer and fasting, but if you fail to honor your wife in a way that she feels honored, I won't hear your requests. On the other hand, if you treat this daughter of mine well— watch out, because I *love* to answer such a godly man's prayers!"

Not really much of a choice, is it? I say, choose understanding. Choose honor. And choose influence with God.

+   MARRIAGE BUILDER

> It is a lifelong project to learn to understand each other. But only in understanding is true love. If you can figure out the person with whom you are living, everything else will be easy by comparison. CAROLE MAYHALL[27]

submission is a two-way street

Be filled with the Spirit, . . . submitting to one another in the fear of God.
EPHESIANS 5:18, 21 (NKJV)

NO HUSBAND SHOULD TALK to his wife about submitting to him (à la Ephesians 5:22) until he has first read Ephesians 5:21, where God calls for *mutual* submission. Isn't it interesting that before God says a word to wives or husbands individually, he first instructs *couples* to submit to one another in the fear of God.

The Greek word translated *submit* here means "to get in order under something." In a military sense, it means "to rank beneath" or "to rank under." It can also be translated "to support one another." Husbands and wives are to support one another in the fear of God.

A husband's biggest booster and most ardent supporter should be his wife. A wife's greatest encourager and most ardent supporter should be her husband. They need to support one another in the reverence of God. Husbands must undergird their wives and hold them up, and wives must do the same for their husbands. Both partners should always be ready to meet their spouse's needs and to sacrifice their own desires to help meet those of their mate. This is not to imply that a husband abdicates his responsibility for leadership in the home in his submission to his wife. Yet it does help to explain what submission is all about.

This issue is not about superiority or inferiority; it is about mutual

49

sacrifice. It is about placing the needs of your mate above your own. Most importantly, it is about imitating God and walking in love.

The husband no more "possesses" his wife than she "possesses" him. He is not superior; she is not inferior. They belong to each other. Therefore, when God calls a wife to submit to the leadership of her husband, He is not saying that the woman is any less than the man. She most definitely isn't.

First Corinthians 7:3-4 shows beautifully how mutual submission really amounts to a true partnership between a husband and wife. "Let the husband render to his wife the affection due her, and likewise also the wife to her husband," writes the apostle Paul. "The wife does not have authority over her own body, but the husband does. And likewise the husband does not have authority over his own body, but the wife does" (NKJV).

There it is again—a delightful partnership. No godly husband can say to his wife, "You do what I say"; and no godly wife can speak with a reciprocal arrogance. God calls both husbands and wives to see themselves in a partnership together. That means working together and submitting to—and supporting—one another out of reverence to God.

+ MARRIAGE BUILDER

Mutual submission is having a task so gigantic that everyone must pull together using whatever muscle, strength, and ingenuity is available in order to get the task done. KAREN MAINS[28]

The Motive and Manner of submission

Wives, submit to your own husbands, as to the Lord.

EPHESIANS 5:22 (NKJV)

THE APOSTLE PAUL DOESN'T instruct wives merely to submit to their husbands and leave it at that; he also gives them a *motive* and a *manner* of submitting.

The motive of submission is obedience to God, and the manner of submission is "as to the Lord." Wives are to submit to their husbands, *as if* they were doing so to the Lord Himself. God instructs wives to submit to their husbands as an act of submission to Christ.

Colossians 3:23 echoes the same idea: "Whatever you do, do it heartily, as to the Lord and not to men" (NKJV). This passage doesn't apply specifically to a wife submitting to her husband; instead, it applies to all of us. We are all to submit to those in authority over us, whether to employers, teachers, law enforcement personnel, or others. "Everyone must submit himself to the governing authorities, for there is no authority except that which God has established. The authorities that exist have been established by God," Paul writes in Romans 13:1. "Give everyone what you owe him: If you owe taxes, pay taxes; if revenue, then revenue; if respect, then respect; if honor, then honor" (v. 7).

We may not always appreciate what someone in authority asks us to do, but we should respond according to the following principle: "What would I do if it were Jesus asking me to do this?"

Your boss might say, "I want you to go and move those boxes." You might immediately think, *Get somebody else to move those boxes. I don't want to. Besides, I am on a break.* But if you put Jesus into the equation, then you will move those boxes; in fact, you will get to work both quickly and happily. Why? Because as a Christian, you take joy in doing whatever the Lord commands you.

Wives, think of submission like this. Let's say you receive a knock at your door. You look to see who it is, and you find Jesus standing there. When you open the door to let Him in, the Lord walks into your kitchen and says, "I am a little hungry. Could you fix Me a bite to eat?" Would you say, "Jesus, I'm kind of busy. Why don't You just make it Yourself"? Of course not. I'm sure you would say, "Lord, I will make You whatever you want. In fact, it would be my privilege to make You a gourmet feast! Let me get Martha Stewart on the phone."

The key is, you want to do your very best for Him. Why? Because He is Jesus and you love Him. This is what God is saying to you in this passage on submission. Submit to your husband as to the Lord. Do it as an act of worship to Jesus Christ. That changes things, doesn't it?

+   MARRIAGE BUILDER

In obeying her husband, the Christian wife is obeying the Lord who has sanctioned the marriage contract. It should be noted that all Paul says is within the context of a Christian marriage. He is not implying that women are inferior to men or that all women should be subject to men. The subjection, moreover, is voluntary, not coerced. The Christian wife who promises to obey does so because her vow is "to the Lord." A. SKEVINGTON WOOD[29]

27

The Model of Submission

Then He went down with them and came to Nazareth, and was subject to them. LUKE 2:51 (NKJV)

FALLEN HUMAN NATURE NATURALLY resists the idea of voluntarily "submitting" to anyone. We tend to think—and our culture reaffirms—that submission implies inferiority.

But if this were true, then how are we to explain the voluntary submission of Jesus Christ during His earthly life? The fact is, Jesus often submitted Himself to human authority. He humbled Himself and thereby provided us with a perfect model of submission.

At age twelve, Jesus went with His parents to Jerusalem to celebrate a feast. When it came time to return home, His parents incorrectly assumed He had joined other family members or friends headed for Nazareth. When they could find Him nowhere among the pilgrims, they returned to Jerusalem—and found Him in the temple, astonishing all the teachers with insightful questions and answers. Mary mildly rebuked her son for His absence, and He replied, "Did you not know that I must be about My Father's business?" (Luke 2:49, NKJV). Nevertheless, Luke says, "He went down with them and came to Nazareth, *and was subject to them.*"

Even at this young age, Jesus clearly knew His role in God's program for the world. He called the God of heaven, "My Father," and never suffered from the least feeling of inferiority. Yet He made Himself "subject" to Mary and Joseph as those placed in authority over Him.

And remember the scene years later when Jesus met His disciples in the upper room? He took off His outer garment, got down on His hands and knees, and began to wash their feet. Did that mean He felt inferior to them? Did that mean they deserved such treatment? No—far from it. He even washed the feet of Judas, who He knew would shortly betray Him. In other words, He voluntarily submitted to His disciples.

Nor did His submission end in the upper room. He submitted Himself to those who arrested Him in Gethsemane, even though they fell to earth at the mere mention of His true identity (John 18:6). He submitted Himself to the interrogation of the high priest, even though He had descended from heaven and ruled in the true temple of God (John 3:13, 31-33). He submitted Himself to the authority of Rome, even though He could have called upon twelve legions of angels to wipe them off the face of the earth (Matthew 26:53). And at the end of history, Jesus will voluntarily submit Himself to the rule of the Father (1 Corinthians 15:28).

Submission is not a dirty word; Jesus proves that beyond all doubt. We are all called to submit to God and to one another, and wives are instructed to submit to their husbands. If you put God at the forefront and submit as unto Him, your marriage can be the delight God intends it to be.

+ MARRIAGE BUILDER

Jesus wears a sovereign crown but bears a father's heart. He is a general who takes responsibility for his soldiers' mistakes. But Jesus didn't write a note, he paid the price. He didn't just assume the blame, he seized the sin. He became the ransom. He is the general who dies in the place of the private, the King who suffers for the peasant, the Master who sacrifices himself for the servant. He is the Son of Man who came to serve and to give his life as a ransom . . . for you. MAX LUCADO[30]

the Limits to submission

Wives, submit to your husbands, as is fitting in the Lord. COLOSSIANS 3:18

IF WIVES ARE TO submit to their husbands "as is fitting in the Lord," does that mean they are to obey all demands, even those that violate the wife's conscience or the Word of God?

No, it doesn't. If a husband were to ask his wife to do something unscriptural, God calls the wife to respectfully decline. As Peter and the other apostles replied to those who demanded that they stop preaching in the name of Jesus, "We must obey God rather than men!" (Acts 5:29).

But let's get practical. Clearly, if your husband asks you to do something immoral or unethical, you should feel under no biblical constraint to agree, because the request clearly violates Scripture.

Yet suppose your husband replies, "I want you to go along with me. After all, your Bible says you are supposed to submit to your husband!"

"Yes," you could then reply, "but it also adds the phrase 'as is fitting in the Lord'—and this just isn't fitting. You are asking me to do something that dishonors God, and I cannot do that."

Always remember that God never asks a Christian wife to violate, in the name of submission, what His Word clearly teaches. Nor would He ask you to stand around and be a punching bag for some abusive man.

On the other hand, when the request remains reasonable, you are to submit. Of course, I don't think there's anything wrong with occasionally reminding your husband of the great responsibility of leadership. Your husband may say, "I want to buy a new (fill in the blank)." You could respond, "Dear, you know that we are really not in a position to do that this month. I have been looking over our finances. We just don't have the resources. Maybe we should wait a little while?"

"No," he may argue. "We are going to do it *now.*" If he refuses to budge, you can wash your hands of the matter by saying, "Okay, dear. But you are going to stand before God Almighty one day to give an account for this decision. If you believe the Lord is leading you to do this as the head of this home, we are with you." Don't be surprised if he later says (after storming out and slamming a couple of doors), "I changed my mind."

There is nothing wrong with a wife reminding her husband of his responsibilities. There is nothing wrong with her offering her input and telling her husband what she thinks—and any reasonable husband will welcome it.

Just keep in mind, wives, that God will never ask you to submit if that means violating what the Bible teaches. In that case, you can refuse with a clear conscience. There are limits to submission.

+ MARRIAGE BUILDER

The husband does not replace Christ as the woman's supreme authority. She must never follow her husband's leadership into sin. But even where a Christian wife may have to stand with Christ against the sinful will of her husband, she can still have a spirit of submission. She can show by her attitude and behavior that she does not like resisting his will and that she longs for him to forsake sin and lead in righteousness so that her disposition to honor him as head can again produce harmony. JOHN PIPER[31]

without a word

WOMEN TEND TO BE more verbal than men. Although there are exceptions to the rule, women generally speak more words than men do. I've seen this play out in the way men and women answer the phone. When a man answers the phone, he reaches for a pencil. When a woman answers the phone, she reaches for a chair!

There is a limit, however, to what words can accomplish. The apostle Peter says that unbelieving husbands are more easily won to the Lord by the way their Christian wives *live,* than by what they say. A woman named Janice made that discovery with her own husband:

For more than ten years, my husband was in bondage to drugs. There never was a dull day. I never knew if my husband was going to be home when I got home from work, if he was going to be gone for a day or a week, if he would get busted, if he was going to get some sleep, or if he would die that day.

I tried to control my husband's actions, questioned him a lot, and tried to get him to spend more time with me. I was running myself ragged. I then read 1 Peter 3:1-2. As women, it is hard to keep our mouths quiet.

But God helped me to stop nagging and questioning my husband and to let Him take care of him.

I remember how he had been gone a couple of days, and I didn't know where he was. I was worried about him. When I heard him pull up in the driveway, my heart was racing and I was mad. But I stopped and asked the Lord to help me right away, to calm me and show me what to do. The minute that front door opened, I had a calm voice and told him hello and that I missed him, and I asked him if he wanted something to eat. He told me that he knew I had a right to be mad and to lay into him when he came home. He could handle that. But when I would be kind and not blow up, he couldn't handle that. He said, "How do you fight kindness?"

Because this woman hung onto God's Word and did what it told her to do, she can testify, "I am proof that it works. My husband told me that the kind of life I lived is what made him decide to follow Christ." She describes the last two and a half years as "glorious" and says that today her husband "loves the Lord and me like I never thought possible."

God knows what He's talking about, doesn't He?

+ MARRIAGE BUILDER

The ancient philosopher Zeno once said, "We have two ears and one mouth, therefore we should listen twice as much as we speak." A wife who follows this advice will not only be obeying God's command to be quick to hear but will be coming one step closer to really loving her man. LINDA DILLOW[32]

ınward and
outward Beauty

Wives, . . . do not let your adornment be merely outward—arranging the hair, wearing gold, or putting on fine apparel—rather let it be the hidden person of the heart, with the incorruptible beauty of a gentle and quiet spirit, which is very precious in the sight of God. 1 PETER 3:1-4 (NKJV)

ALTHOUGH IT'S NEVER WISE to emphasize outward appearance at the expense of the inner life, neither should wives neglect the outside while nurturing the inside.

The word the apostle Peter uses here for "adornment" comes from the Greek term *kosmos,* from which we get our English word *cosmetic.* Peter warns women to avoid focusing on physical appearance to the detriment of the soul.

It is interesting to look at old engravings from the Roman era. The women had amazing hairdos. They would pile their tresses high into towering coiffures, interwoven with golden braids. They wore gold rings on every finger and attached gold all over their clothes. Peter paints a picture here of a woman who flaunts her wealth; the phrase "putting on fine apparel" means the frequent changing of attire. He warns against a woman deliberately dressing in such a way as to be noticed in the church assembly, thus prompting men to gaze on her body instead of worshiping God. Peter is saying, "Concentrate on the inner woman."

At the same time, women should not completely neglect their outward appearance. This passage warns against focusing on the outward; in other words, strike a balance. The Bible certainly does not forbid a woman to present herself in an attractive way. Looking sloppy and unkempt is no virtue—and it can be detrimental to one's marriage.

Anne Graham Lotz, daughter of Billy and Ruth Graham, was interviewed about her parents' love and affection for one another. She told about one visit over a Mother's Day weekend: "Even though mother is almost eighty and has just undergone her fourth hip replacement surgery, when she heard that Daddy was on his way to see her that morning, she got up from her wheelchair, asked me to help her put on a new dress, and fixed up her hair and makeup."[33] Even though Ruth Graham has reached her twilight years, she still puts a high priority on looking her best for her husband.

Wife, you can do the same. Make it easy for your man to keep on staring at you by working with the beauty God gave you. When you take the time to fix yourself up for your husband, you are giving him the unspoken message, "You are special to me. I value you enough to take the time to look attractive to you." (By the way, husbands, this is a two-way street!)

Be the most attractive woman you can be, placing your greatest attention on cultivating the beauty within.

+ MARRIAGE BUILDER

The most beautiful of all women seem to have in common some timeless qualities of beauty—grace, wisdom, thoughtfulness, kindness, compassion—and they carry them with a certain sense of confidence. These are the qualities of what I believe to be true beauty. They are accessible to every woman. We need only to put them on and live our lives sheathed in their presence. ALDA ELLIS[34]

A Remarkable Letter

Your beauty . . . should be that of your inner self, the unfading beauty of a gentle and quiet spirit, which is of great worth in God's sight. 1 PETER 3:3-4

NOT LONG AGO AT my church, I asked to hear from wives who had applied the truths of Scripture and had subsequently seen their husbands turn around spiritually. One letter I received came from a husband who wanted to praise his wife for her steadfast commitment to him during difficult times. Her commitment to honoring God by honoring her husband worked wonders in their home:

> I'm writing this to tell you of the profound effect my wife has had in bringing me home to Jesus. Like many people, I was introduced to the Lord at an early age, having attended Sunday school as a child. As I grew up, I thought of myself as a Christian, but I was what you might call a 'foul weather' Christian—most often the Lord heard from me only when things were going bad and I needed His help. While I had faith and 'believed' in the Lord, you wouldn't know it by my lifestyle.
>
> In the early years of our marriage, my wife, Cindy, found out about Harvest Christian Fellowship and coaxed me into attending. While I routinely resisted coming to church and still hadn't made any significant changes in my life, my wife kept faithfully prodding me on, encouraging me to move forward in my faith and leave my old nature behind.

She never wavered in her love and support—even when I was a creep and became resentful.

Over the last two-plus years, I've made truly significant strides in my walk with the Lord. Putting my old nature behind me was like bringing down a mountain with sandpaper, but the further along I get, the easier it becomes. I find I no longer strongly desire the things of this world and I am happiest when I am in His will.

We are in His Word every day and are a strong, devoted, Christian family. I now look forward to occasions of fellowship. Because of my wife's love, persistence, and devotion to me, I'm happier than I've ever been in my life. I know that God has predestined me to His service, but I cannot help but hold back a little of my gratitude for this beautiful, wonderful person that He predestined me to spend my life with. Thanks to the grace of the Lord, I'll have all eternity to share my gratitude with her.

What a tremendous letter! That grateful husband's words speak a beautiful tribute to a wife who now truly has a *partner* in the faith. This is what can happen when a wife chooses to obey God's instruction and woos her husband with a gentle and quiet spirit.

+ MARRIAGE BUILDER

The heart's beauty is timeless. It can do what no lipstick, powder, miracle cream, or even facelift can do. It creates a glowing fire from within that radiates the smile on a woman's face, illuminates the sparkle in her eyes, and warms the glow in her cheeks. ALDA ELLIS[35]

32

Honor God in All Things

So whether you eat or drink or whatever you do, do it all for the glory of God.
1 CORINTHIANS 10:31

HARRY AND MIRIAM TAYLOR have been happily married for sixty-five
years, spending most of that time on the mission field in places such as
Vietnam and Lebanon. During their decades together they have suffered
through sickness, prison camps, war, and uncertainty. Yet they hung in
there together. And yes, they are still "in love," as Miriam puts it, after all
these years. They still thoroughly enjoy each other's company.

What is their secret?

"As a wife," Miriam says, "there are three little words I like to hear
frequently from my husband: *I love you.* These words are very important to
me, and they give a solid base. I must add that I often tell him 'I love you,' as
well—sometimes even before he has a chance to say it to me. Also an occa-
sional 'I'm sorry' helps me put a lot of things in proper perspective."

Miriam goes on to describe the practical outworking of a Christ-
centered marriage: "There is great strength in a couple's unity of purpose
to honor God in all things. This brings to the front the necessity of praying
together regularly—not only praying together, but working together to bring
about solutions to life's inevitable problems. Happiness in marriage is a
choice. We have found that it is better to discuss matters rather than to
argue. This procedure often ends in laughter. Then, as we make our decisions using God's principles as our guide, it results in having the fruit of the

Spirit: Love is present instead of pent-up anger; joy is evident rather than self-inflicted depression; and peace is manifested instead of the usual anxiety."

Your mate is a gift from God. As such, work on loving your husband or wife as the unique person he or she is. You cannot make your mate into what you want him or her to be. But you can help your spouse to be all that God wants him or her to be. The longer you walk with your mate, the closer you will come to finding the pleasure of living every day together.

Would you like to have a marriage like the one Miriam and Harry enjoy? Then spend time aggressively developing friendship and romance in your marriage. The more time you spend cultivating these things, the less time (and interest) you will have in seeking them elsewhere. The Taylors' long and successful marriage proves that following Christ's design for intimacy between a husband and a wife produces a security, love, and fulfillment that cannot be found anywhere else.

+   MARRIAGE BUILDER

God is still in the business of creating marriages. He desires to be the foundation stone of each union. Most marriages are based on nothing; it is not surprising that many collapse. But it is never too late with God. At any point, if we turn over our lives and our marriages to Him, He will become the foundation, the builder, and the rebuilder, if that is necessary, of that home. Even the broken pieces of our lives can be mended and repaired if we let God be God in every area of our human relationships. JACK MAYHALL[36]

33

The cancer of selfishness

Do nothing out of selfish ambition or vain conceit, but in humility consider others better than yourselves. Each of you should look not only to your own interests, but also to the interests of others. PHILIPPIANS 2:3-4

WHILE OUR FAMILY WAS vacationing in Hawaii a few years ago, I read in the *Honolulu Advertiser* the bizarre story of a woman who sacrificed her family to the whims of selfishness.

One day Katherine Jacobs[37] decided to just "bail out" on her life as a wife and mother of two young sons, ages four and fifteen months. While on vacation with her husband, a family emergency back home necessitated her premature return—but instead, on a lark, she decided to spend a few days on the island of Maui.

The article said she went surfing, sailing, and horseback riding. Strangers took her to restaurants. She sang karaoke. Eventually three people in a townhouse invited her to move in, and she did.

To explain her behavior she told a reporter, "You know what the term 'free spirit' means? That's what I am now. Now I view things from a different light."

Jacobs had been reading a lot of books, such as *The Way of the Wizard: Twenty Spiritual Lessons for Creating the Life You Want* by Deepak Chopra. She said she felt the influence of many mass media messages, from Oprah Winfrey to Forrest Gump. Her new philosophy is, "You have to lose yourself to see yourself. You have to let go of all the stuff going on around you before you can see clearly."

Apparently for Katherine Jacobs, "losing herself" and "letting go of all the stuff" meant abandoning her husband and her marriage—which she acknowledged was pretty good—along with her two little boys.

"For me this is something I had to do," she explained. "I am a better mother and will be a better mother when I return." At the time the article appeared, her family had asked her to come home, but she said she "wasn't ready yet," because she claimed to be "evolving" and was "still having too much fun." Finally she gave this little pearl of wisdom: "If you are going to take a journey, you might as well have a good time."

In contrast, the Bible teaches that Christian husbands and wives are to focus on the needs of others. We are to put God first, the needs of our mate second, and our own needs third.

If you are a child of God, the Bible teaches that He has given you a new nature (see 2 Corinthians 5:17). And with that new nature, He has given you the power to combat the poison of selfishness: "And I am sure that God, who began the good work within you, will continue his work until it is finally finished on that day when Christ Jesus comes back again" (Philippians 1:6, NLT).

+ MARRIAGE BUILDER

The irony is that self-centeredness often produces the opposite of what we desire. I am actually the biggest obstacle to my own self-fulfillment. The more I concentrate on me—on my needs, my desires, my happiness—the less likely I am to find what I want. AL JANSSEN[38]

34

The Battle of the sexes

Your desire will be for your husband, and he will rule over you. GENESIS 3:16

WHAT STARTED OUT IN a beautiful garden ended up on a wrestling mat. And that's where we remain to this day.

Ever since Adam and Eve disobeyed God and ate the forbidden fruit, their descendants have struggled with what has been called "the battle of the sexes." Left unchecked, our fallen human nature escalates marital battles into full-blown wars.

Genesis 3 gives us some valuable insight into the nature of the male-female battle. The word translated *desire* means "to compel, to impel, or to seek control over." The same word is used in Genesis 4:7 where God says to Cain, "Sin is crouching at your door; it desires to have you, but you must master it." In essence, God was telling Cain, "Sin wants to control you, but you must control it."

The context of these two verses, therefore, tells us that the word *desire* describes something not good. It represents an impulse to control or take power over someone. Sin caused the woman to desire to usurp the place of her husband's headship.

I've known some men who have tried to take this verse about a man ruling over his wife and use it as a proof-text to force their wives to do whatever they demand. This is biblically incorrect. Remember, the passage deals with the result of the curse. When God says that man will rule over the woman, He is not advocating the practice. Instead, He is describing what will happen as a result of man's new sinful nature.

The word translated *rule* here could be rendered, "to have dominion over." It implies authoritarianism and is not the same word used to describe man's dominion over the animal kingdom. Essentially it describes a man wanting to control a woman, the abuse of man's proper authority. With the curse came a distortion of a woman's proper submissiveness and a man's proper authority. This is where the battle of the sexes began, and it has raged ever since.

The roots of both militant feminism and male chauvinism can be traced to this sad moment. Woman has the sinful inclination to dominate a man and usurp his authority, while man has a sinful inclination to put a woman under his feet. Both are equally wrong.

Some will use a verse like this to support what the Bible does not. Others use such a misinterpretation to excuse their disbelief in the Bible. In reality, they haven't sufficiently studied the matter to understand what Scripture really teaches.

In short, the Bible doesn't command the battle of the sexes; it merely predicts it. Only in Christ can husbands and wives overcome their natural inclination for marital warfare and instead create homes of peace, joy, and hope.

+ MARRIAGE BUILDER

We remember the ideal design. It is an extraordinary human faculty, that we can remember even back to the beginning. Even when we cannot see it, we know the ideal and yearn for it . . . the Lord Jesus entered the world to redeem its reality, and to forgive. By forgiveness the same Lord Jesus can enter a marriage, to redeem a relationship. WALTER WANGERIN, JR.[39]

avoid temptation

I made a covenant with my eyes not to look lustfully at a girl. JOB 31:1

JOB HAD A HEALTHY respect for the seductive nature of temptation. Consequently, he made a wholehearted commitment to God to overcome his evil inclinations.

Job's covenant with his eyes can still instruct us today. Guys, when you see a beautiful woman at the office and your mind begins to wander, it's up to you to say, *No. I am not going to do that.* At that moment, you need to turn your gaze and thoughts to something else.

Women, let's say you see a handsome hunk on the beach. You feel tempted to keep looking in hopes that he will quickly steal a glance your way and smile. Instead, you should "pull a Job" and remind yourself, *I'm not going to allow myself to do that.*

Although none of us can always avoid running into temptation, we can keep it from becoming a lustful thought. I can't stop an impure thought from knocking at the door of my imagination, but I don't have to open the door and say, "Come on in and make yourself at home!" What I do with that temptation is up to me. As the saying goes, "You cannot stop a bird from flying over your head, but you can stop one from building a nest in your hair."

Let's say that you go over to a vending machine to buy a can of Coke. It's priced at one dollar. You reach into your pocket and find four quarters. If you put in one quarter and push the button, will the Coke come out? No. How about two quarters? Nope. How about three quarters? Still not enough. Only when you put in all four quarters will the Coke pop out.

Likewise, it takes four quarters, so to speak, to end up in a sinful sexual situation or encounter. Maybe you put in the first quarter by watching pornography. You put in the next quarter by placing yourself in a vulnerable position. You put in the third quarter by spending time with "that" girl or guy. And when you drop in the fourth quarter, it's all over with.

When we give in to temptation, we mustn't shake our fist and blame God for our fall. We can't even blame the devil alone. Sure, he played a part in it, but the fact is that Satan needs our cooperation. In reality, we do this to ourselves. As James wisely says, "Each one is tempted when he is drawn away by his own desires and enticed. Then, when desire has conceived, it gives birth to sin; and sin, when it is full-grown, brings forth death" (James 1:14-15, NKJV).

Follow Job's example and make a covenant with your eyes. Determine ahead of time to resist temptation. And keep those quarters in your pocket—all four of them.

+   MARRIAGE BUILDER

A one-woman kind of man must have a predetermined plan fixed in his mind so he can withstand the sneak attacks of the enemy. We never know when we are going to be tempted with our eyes. That's why the plan must be predetermined. We must anticipate a tempting situation in advance and decide beforehand how we will deal with it. STEVE FARRAR[40]

36

A time to run

Flee also youthful lusts. 2 TIMOTHY 2:22 (NKJV)

IF BUILDING A STRONG marriage is your goal, you must deal effectively with sexual temptation. The Bible's guideline on this matter is clear: flee!

Say you're at home and channel surfing. Suddenly a sexually suggestive scene comes on. Use that muscle in your finger to change the channel— or better yet, just turn off the TV and do something else.

Or perhaps you are poking around on the Internet when you get spammed with a link in your e-mail that would take you to a pornographic site. Do whatever it takes not to go there. It may require turning off your computer. You might even consider installing some filtering software that would make stumbling into pornography virtually impossible. Take whatever practical steps may be necessary to "flee youthful lusts."

Hebrews 12:1 tells us to "lay aside every weight, and the sin which so easily ensnares us, and let us run with endurance the race that is set before us" (NKJV). How can you practically do this? Well, when you see a movie, don't rely on the rating system alone. Take some time to check out the real content of the film. If you've done that and some spicy scene unexpectedly flashes on the screen, get up and walk out.

Joseph used this strategy in Genesis 39. He didn't walk out of a movie theater, of course, but when Potiphar's wife hit on him, he ran away.

This woman was far from subtle. She would lie down on the bed and say, "Joseph. Come here. Have sex with me now." She did this day in and day

71

out, and I imagine she was a relatively attractive woman. Otherwise it wouldn't have been much of a temptation, would it?

One day as Joseph walked by, she grabbed him and said, "I am not waiting for you anymore," then started to pull him down. Do you know what Joseph did? He ran out of there as fast as his two legs could carry him.

Sometimes running is the best thing you can do. Get yourself out as quickly as possible. The Bible says, "Flee also youthful lusts." Dr. Kenneth Wuest's expanded Greek translation of that verse makes the command even more forceful: "The passions of youth be constantly fleeing from."

I like the word *constantly* here. That one adverb says it all. This is not just a onetime thing. You have to be on your guard, day in and day out. The word *flee* also suggests urgency. When you see news footage of a flaming building, do you ever observe survivors taking their sweet time to escape the burning structure? Of course not! They flee for their lives—and we should do no less when faced with the destructive fire of sexual temptation.

Flee temptation and don't leave a forwarding address!

+ MARRIAGE BUILDER

> Quick feet keep a clean heart. You may need to take your coffee break in a different place. You may need to turn and walk another direction in your hotel lobby. You may need to drive another way to work to avoid that billboard. Whatever. Just flee immorality. STEVEN J. LAWSON[41]

pLow your own FieLd

You shall not commit adultery. EXODUS 20:14

I ONCE HEARD THE story of a small boy who was learning about the Ten Commandments in Sunday school. This little guy was having a hard time understanding the meaning of the seventh commandment, "Thou shalt not commit adultery." In fact, he totally misunderstood what his teacher said. When he got home he asked his dad, "Daddy, what does it mean when the Bible says, 'Thou shalt not commit agriculture?'"

Without missing a beat, the father wisely replied, "Son, that just means you are not supposed to plow the other man's field."

That father had it exactly right. His response echoes the wisdom found in Proverbs 5:15: "Drink water from your own cistern, running water from your own well." To stay within these God-given boundaries brings joy and fulfillment, a clear conscience and a spring in one's step. To disregard them brings grief and emptiness and a devastating sense of guilt.

"Marriage should be honored by all, and the marriage bed kept pure, for God will judge the adulterer and all the sexually immoral," says Hebrews 13:4. The apostle Paul adds, "It is God's will that you should be sanctified: that you should avoid sexual immorality; that each of you should learn to control his own body in a way that is holy and honorable, not in passionate lust like the heathen, who do not know God; and that in this matter no one should wrong his brother or take advantage of him. The Lord will punish men for all such sins, as we have already told you and warned you" (1 Thessalonians 4:3-6).

At the same time, let's remember something very simple that I think we often forget: God created sex to be fully enjoyed within marriage. Some people envision God saying, "I hate sex. I hate it when people engage in it. It is evil and vile." No, it isn't. God doesn't hate sex. He created it as an expression of the love that husbands and wives are to share. God gave us all a sexual drive. Sex is not bad or evil, but is one of the Lord's most gracious gifts when enjoyed in its proper context.

And guess what? God even delights in blessing sex. That's what the Bible declares in Proverbs 5:18 when it says to husbands, "May your fountain be blessed, and may you rejoice in the wife of your youth."

To experience that blessing, however, you must be married to the person with whom you are sexually intimate. God will never, under any circumstance, bless sex outside of marriage. But within marriage? Now that's another story!

+ MARRIAGE BUILDER

> How can anyone say God thought sex was wrong or dirty when He, the almighty Creator of the universe, said our physical oneness is to be a picture of the spiritual oneness He wants to have with us? It's as if God is saying, "Through your lovemaking, I've given you a visual picture so that when you experience the beauty of physical intimacy, you will have a glimmer, an earthly idea, of all I desire for you spiritually, a sweet union of your spirit with mine." Such glorious oneness is almost beyond comprehension. LINDA DILLOW AND LORRAINE PINTUS[42]

serious business

We should not commit sexual immorality, as some of them did—and in one day twenty-three thousand of them died. 1 CORINTHIANS 10:8

OF ALL THE SINS a man or woman may commit, adultery seems to carry some of the biggest consequences. Sexual unfaithfulness in marriage destroys trust, and without trust, no marriage can prosper.

Perhaps this is why God makes such a big deal out of adultery. He hates all sin, of course, but He seems especially to loathe adultery. So He says in Leviticus 20:10, "If a man commits adultery with another man's wife—with the wife of his neighbor—both the adulterer and the adulteress must be put to death." The New Testament takes note of this divine anger and says in 1 Corinthians 10:8 that twenty-three thousand Israelites died in a single day after sinning sexually.

Proverbs 6:32 tells us, "A man who commits adultery lacks judgment; whoever does so destroys himself." And the gentle Jesus, speaking of a woman he calls Jezebel, tells the church of Thyatira, "I have given her time to repent of her immorality, but she is unwilling. So I will cast her on a bed of suffering, and I will make those who commit adultery with her suffer intensely, unless they repent of her ways" (Revelation 2:21-22).

Adultery is a big deal to God.

"Flee from sexual immorality," writes the apostle Paul. "All other sins a man commits are outside his body, but he who sins sexually sins against his own body. Do you not know that your body is a temple of the Holy Spirit, who is in you, whom you have received from God? You are not your own; you were bought at a price. Therefore honor God with your body" (1 Corinthians 6:18-20).

I have heard some men who were unfaithful to their wives say that it didn't mean anything, that it really was no big deal. They say to their wronged mates, "Hey, it was only a one-night stand. Don't you know that I love you? She meant nothing to me."

But adultery is a big deal. The Bible says that those who become sexually involved become one, even if the union occurs with a prostitute (see 1 Corinthians 6:16). Even if the adultery lasts only a few seconds, it violates the oneness a husband shares with his wife. And that always displeases the Lord, as King David discovered when he committed adultery with Bathsheba. The Bible says simply of his act, "But the thing David had done displeased the Lord" (2 Samuel 11:27). And for the rest of his life, David reaped the consequences of that divine displeasure.

There really is no such thing as "casual sex"—no matter what our society might say. God declares this to be a serious issue, and we trifle with it at our own peril.

+ MARRIAGE BUILDER

This powerful thing that God created is not simple. It is a complex and wonderful gift that we cannot easily conform to our own requirements. We can't have it both ways—at least not very well. We can't worship sex and at the same time treat it casually. We can't deny the bounds of morality and hope to preserve our integrity. We can't pursue unrestrained sexual freedom and hope to avoid the unconscious crafting of our own chains. Our confusion can be resolved only if we look for the truth about sex from the source of all truth. Only then can we begin to make some sense out of the immense mystery of our sexuality. DR. ED YOUNG[43]

make room for forgiveness

The punishment inflicted on him by the majority is sufficient for him. Now instead, you ought to forgive and comfort him, so that he will not be overwhelmed by excessive sorrow. I urge you, therefore, to reaffirm your love for him. 2 CORINTHIANS 2:6-8

SEXUAL SIN CAN DEVASTATE a marriage—but the wonderful grace of God can repair the damage inflicted even by adultery.

As a pastor, I've seen and heard stories of couples who have survived and come through the devastation caused by adultery. One woman wrote to tell me how her marriage was restored after her husband's unfaithfulness:

> *George had an affair when he was in his early forties. We went through hell for three years. I don't think the affair lasted that long, but the hell did. Yet we came out of that crisis and we were one. It was so wonderful. George said that if it got any better, we just couldn't stand it.*

> *Adultery is from the pit of hell. It destroys faith in the partner, security, and love. But if we will allow Him, God can take the ashes and bring such beautiful glory out of it, no one would believe.*

That is a beautiful letter of forgiveness. This woman's husband has since gone on to heaven, but she is left with memories of a relationship restored by God. Her letter bears wonderful testimony to the biblical promises that God can indeed give beauty for ashes, joy instead of mourning, and praise in place of despair (see Isaiah 61:3). Yes, with the help of the Lord, a marriage can survive even the desolation of adultery.

Don't think for a moment, however, that I am excusing this awful sin. God doesn't, and neither should we. Yet there is a difference between a man or a woman who has fallen into adultery but has confessed and repented and wants to make the marriage work, and an unrepentant individual who has hidden a twenty-year affair from his or her spouse. When a young man in Corinth who had committed adultery with his stepmother repented, the apostle Paul told the church to "forgive and comfort him, so that he will not be overwhelmed by excessive sorrow." That ought always to be our attitude toward the truly repentant. On the other hand, it's a whole different ball game with the habitual adulterer who has no intention of changing, even when caught. God Himself will deal with that individual (see Hebrews 13:4).

Bottom line? Even in cases of marital unfaithfulness, divorce is not commanded or mandatory. Jesus says simply that it is permitted (see Matthew 19:8-9). Even if adultery has taken place, every effort should be made to restore the marriage. Remember, immorality is not only grounds for divorce—it is also grounds for forgiveness. If at all possible, we ought to aim toward reconciliation, because God loves to "take the ashes and bring such beautiful glory out of it, no one would believe."

+ MARRIAGE BUILDER

Forgiveness . . . is the single most significant tool we have for meeting and for healing the troubles which marriage shall surely breed between us. What those troubles will be, we do not know. But that they will be, we may be assured. And nothing—neither our love, our effective communication with each other, our talents, our money, nor all the good will in the world—no, nothing can make right again the wrongs as can forgiveness. WALTER WANGERIN, JR.[44]

spend time with the godly

Do not be misled: "Bad company corrupts good character."
1 CORINTHIANS 15:33

MARRIAGE TAKES A MAN and a woman and binds them together as one—but a good marriage requires more than just the husband and wife. The best marriages, while carefully safeguarding the sanctity of the union, also seek out help and encouragement and counsel from godly friends and family members.

Sometimes I hear a puzzled husband or wife wonder aloud, "Why am I being tempted all the time?" In most cases, it's no mystery. When I ask, "Well, with whom have you been spending time?" I often get answers that boil down to something like, "I've just been hanging out and going to parties with a bunch of corrupt people." No wonder temptation comes calling! Such foolish men and women set themselves up to fail.

Because the apostle Paul knew this, right after he tells the young Timothy to flee youthful lusts, he advises him to "pursue righteousness, faith, love and peace, *along with those who call on the Lord out of a pure heart*" (2 Timothy 2:22, italics mine). "Get with the godly," Paul advises. "Spend time with those who delight in walking with the Lord."

Why should the apostle give such advice? It's simple. The kind of company you keep plays a big role in the kind of lifestyle you lead. "Do not be misled," Paul writes, "Bad company corrupts good character."

Scripture consistently warns of the dangers of hanging around those who do not love the Lord. Psalm 1:1-2 says, "Blessed is the man who walks not in the counsel of the ungodly, nor stands in the path of sinners, nor sits in the seat of the scornful; but his delight is in the law of the Lord, and in His law he meditates day and night" (NKJV).

Let me go one step further: if you want your marriage to thrive, you need to spend time with those who actively pursue their walk with the Lord— "those who call on the Lord out of a pure heart." Why would you want to follow the counsel of a halfhearted Christian who doesn't think and act biblically, anyway? You need strong Christian friends in the Lord who will "tell it to you straight" and keep you accountable to Jesus Christ, using God's Word as their source.

So take a good look at the company you keep. Are the men and women who surround you helping you to move forward in your spiritual walk? Or are they pulling you back? Avoid at all costs relationships that appear flirty or friendships that would encourage such activity. If you sincerely want to prevent immorality from banging at your door, you may need to make some changes in the company you keep. Spend time with the godly, and you'll soon begin to discover the "eternal pleasures" to be found only at the right hand of God (see Psalm 16:11).

+ MARRIAGE BUILDER

Our friends and associates can have a profound influence on us, often in very subtle ways. If we insist on friendships with those who mock what God considers important, we might sin by becoming indifferent to God's will. . . . Do your friends build up your faith, or do they tear it down? True friends should help, not hinder, you to draw closer to God. *LIFE APPLICATION STUDY BIBLE*[45]

standing firm in the firestorm

Be on your guard; stand firm in the faith; be men of courage; be strong.
1 CORINTHIANS 16:13

A NUMBER OF YEARS ago, a series of devastating wildfires swept over southern California. Down in the Laguna Niguel area, twenty homes were burned to their foundations. In the midst of all these gutted homes, however, one solitary house resisted the flames. In fact, it escaped virtually unscathed. It suffered only minor discoloration from the smoke that had engulfed the homes on either side of it.

A firefighter at our church who helped to stop that blaze told me that he had taken special note of that lone house after the wildfire had ended. Everyone wondered how this single structure had survived the fire that ravaged the entire neighborhood.

It turned out that the man who built this home went the extra mile in selecting his building materials. He chose to go beyond the basic building requirements in order to make his house safer and essentially fireproof. That included double-paned windows, thick stucco walls, special eaves, a concrete tile roof, and abundant insulation. When the firefighters learned what this homeowner had done, they declared his property a good place to make a stand.

Today our nation desperately needs a good place to make a stand. The wildfire of divorce continues to sweep across our land, consuming home after home in its flaming path. And Christian homes have not been exempt.

Recent statistics suggest that the divorce rate for born-again Christians is slightly *higher* than for those with no faith at all.[46]

Although we cannot stop the wildfire of divorce from running unchecked across our country, we can take steps to fireproof our own homes. We can't stop the flames in the whole culture, but we can stop them at our own doorsteps. And we begin by saying, "The word *divorce* is not going to be a part of my vocabulary. My spouse and I are going to do everything we can to keep our relationship as strong as possible."

We must keep on our guard. We must stand firm in the faith. We must be men and women of courage. We must be strong, especially when we feel the heat of combustible homes catching fire all around us. By depending upon God to supply us abundantly with effective fire-retardant materials—things like earnest prayer and solid Christian fellowship and rich Bible teaching and practical outreach—we, too, can build homes capable of surviving the ravages of the firestorm called divorce. "When the storm has swept by, the wicked are gone," says Scripture, "but the righteous stand firm forever" (Proverbs 10:25).

Don't let divorce reduce your home to ashes. Take the time and effort required to protect your home. Make it divorce-proof. You can turn your home into a good place to make a stand.

+ MARRIAGE BUILDER

Love is not sweeter the second time around. So say the statistics. A 67 percent failure rate for first marriages quickly ascends to a 75 percent failure rate for second marriages and 84 percent for third marriages. We do not learn by our mistakes in marriage; we repeat them. The best chance we will ever have for our happiness and the happiness of our children is to make our present marriage work. GARY RICHMOND AND LISA BODE[47]

42

An act of patriotism

He who fears the Lord has a secure fortress, and for his children it will be a refuge. PROVERBS 14:26

STANDING BY YOUR SPOUSE and children in this day and age is one of the most courageous things you can do. In some respects, you could even say it is an act of patriotism.

I say that because so many of our country's social ills—teen pregnancy and suicide, youth violence, rampant drug abuse—can be traced back to broken homes. We make heroes today out of guys who can drop a ball in a basket or strum four chords on an electric guitar. Talented? Perhaps. Heroic? I really don't think so. It seems to me that their careers entail very little risk and they are well compensated for their efforts.

Heroism isn't using your God-given talents to make yourself a millionaire; rather, it's standing by your commitment to your family. It's placing the needs of others above your own. It's doing what is right regardless of whether it is popular or easy. It's being willing to lay down your life, if necessary, for those you love. To my way of thinking, the true heroes are moms and dads who honor the commitment they made to each other and to their children.

Of course, faithfulness is often hard; but who said the most worthwhile things in life should be easy? When King David described the kind of person who earned his lasting respect, he spoke of an individual "who keeps his oath even when it hurts" (Psalm 15:4). That's what all heroes and patriots do—they keep their word, even when it hurts.

Not only do patriots and heroes say things like, "I regret that I have but one life to give for my country," they also proclaim, "I made a commitment on my wedding day to love this person 'for better for worse, for richer for poorer, in sickness and in health, till death do us part.' And I intend to keep that commitment!"

If you are someone who keeps a commitment even when it hurts, then I salute you as a hero (or at least a hero in the making). The great preacher C. H. Spurgeon put it this way: "A good character is the best tombstone. Those who loved you and were helped by you will remember you. So carve your name on hearts and not on marble."

When we commit ourselves to our spouse and children, we are doing just that—carving our name on living hearts. And by that courageous act we join the ranks of patriots and heroes through the ages.

+ MARRIAGE BUILDER

Jesus Christ is Lord of all who desire to make our homes an outpost of civilization. One day the Lord Jesus is going to come back to this earth. He's coming to settle up. The Lord Jesus Christ not only rides for the brand, He is the brand. His name is above every name and His brand is above every brand. To those of us who have chosen to ride for the brand, and stand for the brand, and fight for the brand, it should be said that of all men, we are most privileged. For it is our honor and our duty to occupy until He comes. STEVE FARRAR[48]

43

Gifts from God

Behold, children are a heritage from the Lord, the fruit of the womb is a reward. PSALM 127:3 (NKJV)

EACH YEAR WHEN Christmas rolls around, many of us dig out our favorite yuletide CDs. Every Christmas I listen to one poignant tune that describes "the best gift" the songwriter ever received. Little by little she describes the gift—and only at the end of the song do we discover that the "gift" is a "tiny, newborn child."

Our culture doesn't very often use the word *gift* to describe children, but that is exactly what they are. The word translated *heritage* in Psalm 127 could also be rendered *gift*. From the viewpoint of heaven, our children are gifts to us from God. They are "precious in His sight," as the old song goes, and they ought to be precious to us as well.

The Gospels make it clear that Jesus loved little children and even went out of His way to make time for them. Many of Jesus' teachings and miracles involved children.

Luke tells us that one day some parents "brought infants to Him that He might touch them; but when the disciples saw it, they rebuked them. But Jesus called them to Him and said, 'Let the little children come to Me, and do not forbid them; for of such is the kingdom of God. Assuredly, I say to you, whoever does not receive the kingdom of God as a little child will by no means enter it' " (Luke 18:15-17, NKJV).

This tender scene with Jesus and the little children reflected a classic

Jewish custom. Fathers would lay their hands on the heads of their children and then lovingly speak a blessing over them. Mark's Gospel adds that Jesus took these children into His arms and began to *fervently* bless them. Without question, He felt passionate about kids!

Interestingly, the disciples did not share His passion. They didn't think of these children as gifts to be treasured but as annoyances to be pushed aside. So they commanded the children's doting parents to back off and take their bothersome kids with them. As soon as the Lord caught wind of it, He indignantly said, "Let them continue to come to me and stop hindering them!" (literal translation).

When Jesus looked into the face of a child, He saw a gift from God. It didn't matter to Him what "wrapping" the child came in—dark skin or light skin, redhead or brunette, blue eyes or brown—the Master loved them all.

These gifts from God are not ours to be molded but rather to be *unfolded.* It is our privilege as parents to help them discover the unique individual that God has made them. We are not to teach our children to depend upon us for the rest of their lives but to depend completely upon God. They may be His gifts to us—but they are still His, after all.

+ MARRIAGE BUILDER

Jesus told us we must become like little children to enter the kingdom. Take some time today to spend with a child. Instead of teaching him, try learning something from him. See if that child can help you to become more childlike.

44

Affirm your children

But encourage one another daily, as long as it is called Today, so that none of you may be hardened by sin's deceitfulness. HEBREWS 3:13

A MAGAZINE ARTICLE THAT appeared many years ago continues to teach me today about the necessity and power of encouraging and affirming my children.

Author Aletha Jane Lindstrom told how one day she ran into a friend and her seven-year-old son standing outside a bakery. "Jimmy brought me," the woman said. "He stops here every morning on his way to school to 'smell the good smells.' I'd forgotten the aroma of baked goods fresh from the oven!"

As the woman spoke, Aletha said her friend's little son squeezed her hand and looked up at his mother, "his eyes shining with pride."[49]

Now, why did that little boy beam with delight? Was it because his mother had spent months creating some masterpiece? No. His heart soared because Mom had listened to his description of the "good smells" at the bakery, had gone out of her normal routine to share the experience with him, and took the time to affirm her son. In those simple moments, he knew he "mattered." And so he beamed.

Every child needs to feel affirmed and loved. Every child needs to hear Mom and Dad's genuine praise. "A word aptly spoken is like apples of gold in settings of silver," says Proverbs 25:11.

Our kids need to hear positive things from us. The words we say can stick with them for a lifetime—but they need more than our words. They also need our ears.

Lindstrom also recalled how, one day on a beach, she watched a young girl "select stones from the water's edge and carry them to her mother. Then they sat, heads together, while the girl happily attempted to identify her treasures. I later commented to the mother, 'You must be tremendously interested in stones.' 'It's Sally's interest,' she replied. 'Right now it's stones. Next month it may be shells or wildflowers. She needs someone to listen.' "[50]

Lindstrom wasn't surprised to learn that Sally was a top student and science expert in her class, and neither am I. It's amazing what can happen when we make affirming our children a priority.

And it's never too late to affirm your kids! Even if your children are grown and out of the house, don't think your influence has stopped. It might surprise you how much it would mean to your adult child if you called today and said something like, "I was just thinking about you and I wanted to tell you that I love you and am very proud of you."

Affirmation knows no age limits, recognizes no chronological boundaries. When Scripture instructs us to "encourage one another daily, as long as it is called Today, so that none of you may be hardened by sin's deceitfulness," the admonition applies even in the family. Maybe *especially* there. So affirm your kids today!

+ MARRIAGE BUILDER

Like an electric circuit with a break in the line, never telling a child he's valuable fails to close the loop and free the current that lights the bulb. Until you complete the circuit with your words, the light of unconditional love will never shine in a child's life. GARY SMALLEY AND JOHN TRENT[51]

train them up

Train up a child in the way he should go, and when he is old he will not depart from it. PROVERBS 22:6 (NKJV)

NO DOUBT PROVERBS 22:6 is the most-quoted verse in the entire Bible on the subject of parenting. As Chuck Swindoll has pointed out, the phrase "train up" originally referred to the actions of a midwife. After delivering a child, she would dip her finger in crushed dates and place that finger in the mouth of the little baby, thus prompting in that child a thirst for milk.

This custom suggests that when we "train up" our children, we need to be internally motivating them instead of externally compelling them. In other words, we need to create a thirst in our children for the things of God.

The verb form of this word speaks of breaking and bringing into submission, like a wild horse with a rope or a bit. In essence, it means setting parameters in our children's lives. We are to establish external boundaries for their protection, but we must also seek to develop an internal motivation for them to know and love the Lord.

Next, we are to train our children in the way that they should go. The word *way* comes from a Hebrew verb form that refers to the "bent" or "bending" of a bow. *The Amplified Bible* version of this verse explains it well: "Train up a child in the way he should go [and in keeping with his individual gift or bent], and when he is old he will not depart from it."[52] Again Chuck Swindoll writes of this term, "In every child God places in our arms, there is a bent, a set of characteristics already established. The bent is fixed and determined before he is given over to our care. The child is not, in fact, a pliable piece of clay. He has been set; he has been bent. And the parents who want to train this child correctly will discover that bent!"[53]

This means that we should fashion our methods of discipline and words of instruction according to that God-given bent. Our goal is to help our children discover God's plan for their lives. Our job is to join them in this journey, using the wisdom from God's Word as our guide—not our own ambitions or emotions.

Finally, we are to train our children in the way they *should* go—not necessarily in the way they *want* to go. The way that they should go is the way of the Lord. Sure, they will resist us at times. But we must remain persistent in our training, committing them to God throughout the process. Then we can rest in the hope that when they are old they will not depart from the delightful way of God—the only way that leads to life, joy, and ultimate satisfaction.

+ MARRIAGE BUILDER

When kids have dilemmas, they often go to parents as their orchard of information. You can take these opportunities to show your child how to decide what to do. And you can use these moments to teach her how to gather information. Be her number one source. You can give out facts and ideas she would never think to consider. Spur her on to Wisdom Thinking. CAROLYN KOHLENBERGER AND NOEL WESCOMBE[54]

setting parameters

And you, fathers, do not provoke your children to wrath, but bring them up in the training and admonition of the Lord. EPHESIANS 6:4 (NKJV)

JUST AS OUR KIDS need our hugs and our affirmation, they also need to know what the parameters are and that they will face consequences for crossing them. The word *training* in Ephesians 6:4 is a strong Greek term that means "discipline even by punishment."

I grew up in a broken home. I lived in all sorts of places—sometimes with my mom, other times with my grandparents. I also attended military school for a number of years, living on campus. Despite feeling horribly homesick and desperately longing to go home, I did learn a number of important things during my "tour of duty" (which seemed more like a prison sentence at the time).

The school was run very much like the military. It did not matter that its residents were children; we still had to wear freshly pressed uniforms every day. We were taught how to get our shoes spit-shined so well we could see our reflection in them. We had a set time to get up in the morning and a set time when the lights went out—no exceptions.

We didn't call the head of our school "the principal"—he was the *general.* We marched in formation with our little rifles. We saluted our commanding officers. I remember a rather tough old woman—we called her the Den Mother—who oversaw the barracks where we slept in our little bunk beds. She wasn't real big on hugs, but she was huge on discipline. When we crossed the line, none of these people fooled around. We were sent to the general, and he would apply the board of education to the seat of under-standing.

I confess that I shaped up real fast. I can still remember a few of my times in the general's office when he pulled out the infamous "cheese paddle," so called because of the holes drilled in its surface, which helped the wood to travel a little faster to its destination.

Cruel, you say? The fact is, with clear rules and ramifications for break-ing them, I flourished. For the only time in my young life, I actually made the honor roll and consistently pulled down A's and B's.

As soon as I went back into the public school system, however, I real-ized how much I could get away with. My grades plummeted. I was constantly in trouble because I knew I would face very few repercussions for my behavior. It was a whole new ball game and I took full advantage of the situation.

Today I see how those tough parameters in military school, as difficult as they seemed at the time, really helped me. I actually flourished in an envi-ronment of discipline.

All children need discipline. This, too, is a way of showing love.

+ MARRIAGE BUILDER

A father is the anchor that God has placed in the life of a child. It is the father's role and responsibility to dig deeply into the solid rock of Christ in order to tether a young boy headed in the wrong direction. Every boy needs the bone-jarring yank that occurs when the anchor takes hold. STEVE FARRAR[55]

ten recommendations

Teach them the right way to live. 1 KINGS 8:36

I ONCE READ ABOUT a pastor who helped out in a correctional center one summer. The center was "home" to a group of young boys whom the system had labeled "incorrigible." This pastor wanted to know why these boys had chosen the course they did.

He asked them to identify some of the problems that might have contributed to their difficult upbringing. He asked them to help him draw up a "code" for parents, zeroing in on specific areas in which their own parents had failed. The young men came up with the following list of ten recommendations:

1. Keep cool. Don't fly off of the handle. Keep the lid on when things go wrong. Kids need to see how much better things turn out when people control their temper.

2. Don't get strung out on booze and drugs. When we see our parents reaching for these crutches, we get the idea that it is perfectly okay to reach for a bottle or a capsule when things get heavy. Children are great imitators.

3. Bug us a little. Be strict. Show us who's boss. We need to know that we have some strong support. When you cave in, we get scared.

4. Don't blow your class. Stay on that pedestal. Don't try to dress, dance, or talk like your kids. You embarrass us and you look ridiculous.

5. Light a candle. Show us the way. God is not dead or sleeping or on

vacation. We need to believe in something bigger and stronger than ourselves.

6. Scare us. If you catch us lying, stealing, or being cruel, get tough. Let us know why what we did was wrong. Impress on us the importance of not repeating such behavior.

7. When we need punishment, dish it out. But let us know you still love us even though we have let you down. It will make us think twice before we do something wrong again.

8. Call our bluff. Make it clear you mean what you say. Don't compromise. Don't be intimidated by our threats to drop out of school or to run away from home. Stand up to us and we will respect you. Kids don't want everything they ask for.

9. Be honest. Tell us the truth no matter what. Be a straight arrow about everything. We can take it. Lukewarm answers make us uneasy. We can smell uncertainty a mile away.

10. Praise us when we deserve it. Give us a few compliments once in a while and we will be able to accept criticism a whole lot easier.

Those kids were basically saying, "Mom and Dad, please do what the Bible says." Young people are looking for parents who will do just what God has told them to do. And that's the very best way to teach our kids the right way to live.

+ MARRIAGE BUILDER

Gold is valuable because it's rare—just like these opportunities to influence our children. Time can be my enemy or my ally. If I don't treat it with the respect it demands, it will rob me of my greatest possessions. TIM KIMMEL[56]

48

Five Reasons for Biblical Discipline

Discipline your son, for in that there is hope; do not be a willing party to his death. PROVERBS 19:18

JOHN MACARTHUR in his excellent book titled *The Family* points out some important principles for raising our children in a godly way. The divinely inspired, time-tested principles of Scripture have helped to rear countless healthy, God-fearing, respectful children through the centuries. Allow me to suggest five reasons from God's Word why you should discipline your children:

1. *Discipline your children to remove foolishness.* Proverbs 22:15 says, "Foolishness is bound up in the heart of a child; the rod of correction will drive it far from him" (NKJV). We may think undisciplined children look "cute," but the Bible warns us they grow up to be "fools."

2. *Discipline your children to rescue them from judgment.* Proverbs 23:13-14 says, "Don't fail to correct your children. They won't die if you spank them. Physical discipline may well save them from death" (NLT). A little discipline now saves a lot of pain later.

3. *Discipline your children to receive wisdom.* Proverbs 29:15 says, "The rod and rebuke give wisdom, but a child left to himself brings shame to his mother" (NKJV). Wisdom comes with a price tag named discipline.

4. *Discipline your child to relieve your anxiety.* Proverbs 29:17 says, "Correct your son, and he will give you rest; yes, he will give delight to your

soul" (NKJV). A little loving discipline applied to the seat of a child usually leads to a lot of peace in the heart of a parent.

5. *Discipline your children so they will reflect God's character.* Hebrews 12:10-11 says, "Our earthly fathers disciplined us for a few years, doing the best they knew how. But God's discipline is always right and good for us because it means we will share in his holiness. No discipline is enjoyable while it is happening—it is painful! But afterward there will be a quiet harvest of right living for those who are trained in this way" (NLT).

Our children need to know there is a God in heaven who loves them and who has a plan and purpose for them—and they need to start hearing of Him very early in their education. The discipline designed by the Lord yields the kind of results we want most; it cannot be improved upon. How could one improve upon the directions supplied by the Manufacturer?

Never look askance at biblical discipline. Modern "experts" may dispute its guidance, but a quick look at our culture reveals what their advice has wrought. The electric chair will never cure crime, but the high chair can. If we truly love our children, we will refuse to withhold appropriate, biblical, loving discipline.

+ MARRIAGE BUILDER

As a parent who has reared four children of my own and as a pastor who has been forced to deal with domestic abuses of every variety imaginable, I have seen both the rewards of fair discipline and the horrors of uncontrolled abuse. There is, admittedly, no way to remove the risk, but in light of the ultimate benefits that accompany the proper discipline of children, I am now more convinced than ever that God honors those who follow His directions. CHARLES R. SWINDOLL[57]

waLk the TaLk

In everything set them an example by doing what is good. TITUS 2:7

OUR CHILDREN MUST SEE the gospel *lived* as well as preached. As followers of Jesus Christ, we are not only to be good examples and witnesses to the outside world; we also need to provide a strong witness in our own homes. Little eyes are watching and little ears are listening. They are paying attention to what really matters to us and how our faith affects our day-to-day living.

In his excellent book on parenting, *Gifts from God,* Dr. David Jeremiah offers this powerful insight:

> A long time ago somebody told me that you never know how good a parent you are until you see your grandchildren. That can be a scary thought, but it can also be a great encouragement. When you live to see your grandchildren standing for the Lord and pressing on in the faith, suddenly all the toil and sweat and uncertainty and difficulties and anxious moments you endured as a young parent seem as nothing compared to the joyous vision that now kisses your eyes.
>
> Christians enjoy the wondrous privilege of passing on their values to their children—but it doesn't happen merely because we profess faith in Christ. It happens when we live out our faith in a winsome and compelling way. When our kids see what a difference Christ makes in our lives, they will want Him to make that same difference in their own.[58]

The books of 1 and 2 Kings show us how important it is to "walk the talk." Listen to these good reports:

- "Asa did what was right in the eyes of the Lord, as his father David had done" (1 Kings 15:11).
- "In everything [Jehoshaphat] walked in the ways of his father Asa and did not stray from them; he did what was right in the eyes of the Lord" (1 Kings 22:43).
- "[Azariah] did what was right in the eyes of the Lord, just as his father Amaziah had done" (2 Kings 15:3).
- "[Jotham] did what was right in the eyes of the Lord, just as his father Uzziah had done" (2 Kings 15:34).
- "[Hezekiah] did what was right in the eyes of the Lord, just as his father David had done" (2 Kings 18:3).

On the other hand, we also read reports like this one: "Amon . . . did evil in the eyes of the Lord, as his father Manasseh had done. He walked in all the ways of his father; he worshiped the idols his father had worshiped, and bowed down to them. He forsook the Lord, the God of his fathers, and did not walk in the way of the Lord" (2 Kings 21:19-22).

Moms and dads, the question you must ask yourself is this: Am I setting a good example for my children?

+ MARRIAGE BUILDER

We communicate more from our life than from our lips. If we want to infect the people around us with the real thing, then our lives need to reflect the very virtue we long for them to embrace. TIM KIMMEL[59]

choose the right path

You shall love the Lord your God with all your heart, with all your soul, and with all your strength. And these words which I command you today shall be in your heart. You shall teach them diligently to your children, and shall talk of them when you sit in your house, when you walk by the way, when you lie down, and when you rise up. DEUTERONOMY 6:5-7 (NKJV)

A FATHER WENT MOUNTAIN climbing with his little boy. Eventually the pair reached a certain point where their climb had become ever more dangerous. As the father pondered which way he should go, he heard the voice of his son behind him.

"Choose the right path, Dad," the little guy said. "I am coming right behind you."

Our own children are saying the same thing to us as we chart our course in life. They are saying, "Choose the right path, Mom. Make the right choice, Dad. I am coming right behind you." They are watching us. They are imitating us.

We cannot instruct our children in the ways of the Lord unless we have first experienced them for ourselves. We must have our own relationship with God. Moses said, "These words . . . shall be in your heart." I cannot lead my child any further than I have come myself. Here's the basic rule: Nothing can happen *through* us until it has happened *in* us.

Are you walking with God? Can you say, as Paul said to his Macedonian friends, "Keep putting into practice all you learned from me and heard from me and saw me doing, and the God of peace will be with you" (Philippians 4:9, NLT)? All of us should be able to ask our sons and daughters to follow the example they have heard from our lips and seen in our lives.

To quote Andrew Murray: "The secret of home rule is self-rule, first being ourselves what we want our children to be." It is hard for parents to train a child in a way those parents haven't first gone themselves.

Teach them diligently, Moses says. This term *diligently* conveys the idea of one object piercing another object, of something that stabs into something else. Your goal as a parent is to penetrate and pierce deeply into the lives of your children, making them keen, sharp, and discerning.

Parents, talk of the things of the Lord when you sit down in your house, when you walk by the way, when you lie down, and when you rise up. Follow the advice of Moses and choose the right path.

+ MARRIAGE BUILDER

Can you think of anything in the entire world more important than for your children to place faith in Jesus Christ and to experience God's wonderful plan for their life? Through prayer, and the model of your own life, you can have confidence that, by God's grace, they will. No man would be unwilling to die for his children. How much more important it is to live for them. PATRICK M. MORLEY[60]

51

A word to Fathers

I write to you, fathers, because you have known him who is from the beginning. 1 JOHN 2:13

NOT SO LONG AGO, child-rearing "experts" were telling us not to worry about the exploding divorce rates because children are very resilient and aren't seriously damaged by broken homes. Besides, they said, kids could grow up just fine without a father.

How times have changed.

Today one could make a case for the importance of the father from secular research alone; you wouldn't even need to quote the Bible. Yet all this research just supports the message of Scripture.

For instance, Harvard University's Sheldon and Eleanor Glueck developed a test (with a 90 percent accuracy rate) to determine which five- and six-year-olds would become delinquent. They discovered four primary factors that keep children from juvenile delinquency:

- The father's firm, fair, and consistent discipline.
- The mother's supervision and companionship.
- The child's parents demonstrate affection for each other and for the child.
- The family spends time together in activities where all participate.[61]

Singer and songwriter Michael W. Smith grew up in a home like that. He says, "I always saw my dad reading the Word. And if he wasn't working and the church doors were open, he was there. Dad didn't talk to me a lot about God, not as much as I do with my kids, but he was dedicated in everything he did. There was never any doubt in my mind about my dad's convictions, because his actions proved them.

"My father really cared about spending time with me. It's real easy in this day and age, when there are so many things to do—especially in a career like mine with demands on your time—to put your own needs before your family's. But my dad always spent time with us. We were a priority in his life."[62]

If fathers weren't significant in the plan of God, the apostle John wouldn't have singled them out as he did in 1 John 2. Fathers, rise to the occasion and respond to this call of God. Be the husband and father that He wants you to be.

"The most important lesson I learned from my dad," Smith continues, "is to remember to say 'I love you' even in the down times. Even when your kids are rebelling, just keep saying it. I'll never forget one particular time when Dad told me he loved me. I'd been down in Nashville, living out of God's will, just breaking his heart. In the middle of this rebellious time, we got on the phone and he told me that he loved me, and I told him that I loved him. I got off the phone and thought, *Man, that's incredible. He told me he loved me. I just pray I can be as consistent with my kids as my dad was with me.*"

Who says kids don't need their fathers?

+ MARRIAGE BUILDER

Fathers are the visible link a child has with God. You will often find that in homes where the father is absent or disengaged and disinterested in a child's life, that child will tend to see the heavenly Father in the same way. Fathers need to be there—nurturing, caring, loving.

52

HOW MUCH DOES DAD KNOW?

Listen to your father, who gave you life.   PROVERBS 23:22

MARK TWAIN SUMMED IT up well when he said, "When I was a boy of fourteen, my father was so ignorant I could hardly stand to have the old man around. But when I got to be twenty-one, I was astonished at how much he had learned in seven years."

Twain's statement reminds me of a clipping someone sent me from a Dutch magazine. It pretty accurately shows the changing attitude of a child toward his parents, especially toward his father, as the years roll by:

At four years old, the child says, "My daddy can do anything."

At seven years, he says, "My daddy knows a lot, a whole lot."

At eight years, he says, "My dad doesn't know everything."

At twelve years, he says, "Naturally, Dad doesn't know that, either."

At fourteen years, "Dad is hopelessly old-fashioned."

At twenty-one years, "That man is so out-of-date."

At twenty-five years, "Dad knows a little bit about that, but not too much."

At thirty years, "I need to find out what Dad thinks about that."

At thirty-five years, "Before we decide, let's get Dad's ideas first."

At fifty years, "What would Dad have thought about that?"

At sixty years, "My dad knew literally everything."[63]

Dear old dad doesn't change that much—but his children do! Sons and daughters just come around to seeing what it's like to be in his position. My friend Tony Evans learned just how much his father knew. There was a time when he didn't think much of his father's rules and discipline. But times changed:

> My father would tell me, "I want you home at 10:00 P.M. That's not 10:01. You be in here at 10:00, or it's fire!" I would get upset and say, "Why do I have to be in here at 10:00? My friends are making fun of me. They can stay out until 2:00 and 3:00 in the morning." And Dad would say, "Well, maybe their parents don't care. But I care. Be in here at 10:00."
>
> When I go back to Baltimore where I grew up, guess where many of those guys are? Still hanging out on the corner until 2:00 and 3:00 in the morning. I can trace where I am today back to a father who had a hold on me, who disciplined me, and who would not let me have my way all the time.

Tony then concludes tellingly, "I'm in love with Jesus Christ today because of it. I didn't get involved in drugs and all of those things the other guys were getting involved in because I had become accountable to my father at home."[64]

Fathers, you know more than you think. And someday your children might even admit it.

+   MARRIAGE BUILDER

Thanks, Dad. If your own father is still living, there is time to speak the words you have waited all of your life to say, and that he has waited all of his life to hear. Please don't wait. Say them loud. Say them clear. Say them now. In the living years. KEN GIRE[65]

53

His Greatest Accomplishment

May your father and mother be glad; may she who gave you birth rejoice!
PROVERBS 23:25

FORMER PRESIDENT GEORGE HERBERT WALKER BUSH was once asked an important question: "What is your greatest accomplishment in life?"

That's a fascinating question to ask someone like George H. W. Bush. After all, he has lived a full and very productive life: U.S. ambassador to China; director of the CIA for a little more than a year; vice president of the United States for two terms under Ronald Reagan; and president of the United States for one term. As commander in chief he oversaw Operation Desert Storm, one of the most effective military campaigns in history. So what do you think he might he say?

Ordinarily I would expect a man of his accomplishments to say something like, "My greatest achievements are my two terms as vice president and one term as commander in chief," or "My greatest accomplishment is that I helped bring about an end to the Cold War."

But his actual answer had nothing to do with any of his political successes. Instead, he summed up his greatest accomplishment with these remarkable words: "My children still come home to see me."[66]

Somehow, in the hurly-burly of an incredibly busy life, George and Barbara Bush must have spent enough significant time with their children that after those kids grew into adulthood, they still looked forward to returning to the Texas ranch to see Mom and Dad. And one of those grown children is now the president of the United States!

Nobody manages such a rich achievement through blind luck. You can bet that, despite their hectic schedules, George and Barbara Bush made time for their children. They didn't continually shuttle them off to caretakers or nannies so they could concern themselves with the "important stuff." Somehow they managed to balance their responsibilities and attack their marriage and parenting challenges in a comprehensive way. They refused to leave their kids behind and so have tasted a little of the goodness the Lord promised through Moses to His people long ago: "Keep his decrees and commands, which I am giving you today, so that it may go well with you and your children after you and that you may live long in the land the Lord your God gives you for all time" (Deuteronomy 4:40).

If we desire to improve our family life, we have to look at the whole package. And that includes our children. The good news is, when we do so, we may well find that our own grown-up kids will want to come home and visit us, too. And that's quite an accomplishment in anyone's portfolio.

+   MARRIAGE BUILDER

Children are our most valuable natural resource. HERBERT HOOVER[67]

on borrowed time

You do not even know what will happen tomorrow. What is your life? You are a mist that appears for a little while and then vanishes. JAMES 4:14

NOT LONG AGO I was reminded that the time we have with our children is really only "borrowed." David, a close friend of mine, had just picked up his ten-year-old daughter, Yvette, to drive her from one birthday party to another. During the trip, the car somehow flipped over, injuring David and killing Yvette.

My heart ached for David and his wife, Yvonne. Cathe and I were very close friends with this couple and their two daughters. Our families had taken vacations together. I had even had the privilege of baptizing Yvette and her eight-year-old sister the previous Thanksgiving. I remember Yvette as a sweet little girl who really loved the Lord.

David was the most doting father you could ever meet. I never saw a father give more attention to a daughter than he did. Nevertheless, David felt wracked with guilt. *If only I had done this. If only I had done that. I wish I had said this more. I wish I had said that more.*

My friend's tragedy made me think of the words of Job when that godly man faced the loss of all his children: "Naked I came from my mother's womb, and naked shall I return there. The Lord gave, and the Lord has taken away; blessed be the name of the Lord" (Job 1:21, NKJV). In the very next verse we read, "In all this Job did not sin nor charge God with wrong" (Job 1:22, NKJV).

As I stood in David's hospital room on the night of the accident, his parents, Hamp and Sue, both committed Christians, came to visit. With his parents standing beside him, David grieved and cried out to the Lord, still struggling with tremendous self-doubt. "David," I said, "you were the greatest father. You loved your daughter." Then I turned to his parents and said, "Mr. and Mrs. Riley, you raised your son in the way of the Lord. He raised his daughter in the way of the Lord. Now she is in the presence of Jesus Christ. You all did your job well!"

David and Yvonne did it right. Although there is no easy way to completely recover from such a tragic loss, think how much worse it would be if David had neglected his daughter—if he had told her he was too busy to bother with her silly parties. Instead, he was there with Yvette in her final moments.

Thankfully, this sorrowing couple had made time for their girls. They had well prepared Yvette for the day when she went to be with the Lord and their "borrowed time" came to an end.

When will our own "borrowed time" run out? None of us knows. Therefore, let's make the most of the time we have with our kids right now.

+ MARRIAGE BUILDER

We took our son Eric too much for granted. Perhaps we all take each other too much for granted. The routines of life distract us; our own pursuits make us oblivious; our anxieties and sorrows, unmindful. The beauties of the familiar go unremarked. We do not treasure each other enough. NICHOLAS WOLTERSTORFF[68]

treasure each moment

Be very careful, then, how you live—not as unwise but as wise, making the most of every opportunity, because the days are evil. EPHESIANS 5:15-16

OH, HOW WE NEED to treasure each moment with our children! At all costs, we must never cause them to question our love. Rather, we should diligently seek out ways to verbalize our affection and care. Why not be generous with our hugs? We might think they feel too old for that, but they may like it more than we think.

Remember David and Yvette, the father and daughter whose tragic story I told in the previous devotion? As they made their last trip together as Daddy and his little girl on this side of heaven, David turned to his sweetheart and said, "I love you."

Yvette looked up at him with her cute little smile and replied, "I love you more!"

The next moment, she was in heaven.

Little Yvette went from the presence of her loving father on earth into the presence of her loving Father in heaven. You couldn't ask for more than that.

"Precious in the sight of the Lord is the death of his saints," says Psalm 116:15. Why is this so? It's because, through the work of Jesus Christ, God has taken the sting out of death. It still hurts us to lose a loved one, even a loved one who walks by faith with Jesus Christ—yet as the apostle Paul could say, "The perishable must clothe itself with the imperishable, and the mortal with immortality. When the perishable has been clothed with the imperishable, and the mortal with immortality, then the saying that is written will come true: 'Death has been swallowed up in victory.' 'Where, O death, is your victory? Where, O death, is your sting?' The sting of death is sin, and the power of sin is the law. But thanks be to God! He gives us the victory through our Lord Jesus Christ" (1 Corinthians 15:53-56).

Months after the accident, David still grieved the loss of his daughter. Yet he did not grieve as those who have no hope, as those who do not know Jesus Christ. David knows that he will see his daughter again—healthy, whole, and fully alive—because she received the same treasure in her heart that he has in his, "namely, Christ, in whom are hidden all the treasures of wisdom and knowledge" (Colossians 2:2-3).

To know that our children will spend eternity with the Lord should be our greatest hope, our shining goal. After all, they are not ours. We don't own them. Sometimes we may think we own them, but in the end we always see that they belong to God. Our aim should be to bring them up in the nurture and admonition of the Lord and to point them to Him. That way, we can treasure every moment we have with them on earth and look forward to even richer times in heaven.

+ MARRIAGE BUILDER

There is no going back. There is no drawing against the "tomorrow." You must live in the present on today's deposits. Invest it so as to get from it the utmost in love, peace, joy, health, happiness, and success! The clock is running. Make the most of today. AUTHOR UNKNOWN

56

No Regret

I have fought the good fight, I have finished the race, I have kept the faith.
Now there is in store for me the crown of righteousness. 2 TIMOTHY 4:7-8

WHEN WE HAD OUR first child, Christopher (now in his mid-twenties), we decided that Cathe should stay at home to be a "hands-on" mom. At the time I was just starting Harvest Christian Fellowship, the church I still pastor.

We were living basically at poverty level. We had no money. We barely had enough food to get through the week. We had no clothes to speak of. All of our furniture came from the Salvation Army or had been given to us by friends. We ate off hand-me-down dishes. We actually had to finance a little black and white television set (we made six-dollar payments each month).

Life was anything but easy—and yet we were able to spend a lot of time with our son in those important formative years of his life. Today I look back on those days and can honestly say I don't regret one single moment. We followed the Lord's will as best we could, and we have no regrets about anything we did.

We get only one chance at life, and once our days are gone, they cannot be retrieved. Therefore it's important to live every day in a way that brings no regrets. So although I've said it before, I'll say it again: Take time for your kids. Don't do anything now that you'll regret later.

Almost a century ago, a man and his son both learned a great deal about regret, but they learned it in very different ways. Against his parents' expressed wishes, William Whitling Borden joined the China Inland

Mission in order to reach the Muslims of northwest China with the gospel of Jesus Christ. Only a few months after he arrived in Asia in 1913, he succumbed to cerebrospinal meningitis and died at the age of twenty-six. His death nearly destroyed his father, the founder of the Borden dairy fortune.

After William's funeral, his grieving father began leafing through a Bible that William had taken to China. Just as Mr. Borden was about to close the Bible's covers forever, he saw a note scrawled on its back flyleaf, written in a familiar hand. Immediately he recognized his son's handiwork and noted a date written next to the words. Mr. Borden, who had never found time for spiritual things, wept as he read the message, written in his late son's own handwriting just one week before he died: "No reserve. No retreat. No regret."

No regret. We need to arm ourselves with that same attitude as we rear our children. God has loaned them to us for a few short years, and when those days are through, we can do no better than to whisper, "No regret."

+ MARRIAGE BUILDER

For of all sad words of tongue or pen,
The saddest are these: "It might have been!" JOHN GREENLEAF WHITTIER[69]

57

Leaving a spiritual Legacy

I have no greater joy than to hear that my children walk in truth.
3 JOHN 1:4 (NKJV)

WHAT GREAT JOY IT brings to parents when their children master the spiritual lessons they have been taught and as a result, want to walk in the way of the Lord. John spoke for all of us when he said, "I have no greater joy than to hear that my children walk in truth."

King David urged his own son to walk in God's truth. On his deathbed, he gave his boy these parting words of wisdom: "As for you, my son Solomon, know the God of your father, and serve Him with a loyal heart and with a willing mind; for the Lord searches all hearts and understands all the intent of the thoughts. If you seek Him, He will be found by you; but if you forsake Him, He will cast you off forever" (1 Chronicles 28:9, NKJV).

Wise and godly parents want to leave their children a spiritual legacy, as the writer of Proverbs says: "My son, if you accept my words and store up my commands within you, turning your ear to wisdom and applying your heart to understanding, and if you call out for insight and cry aloud for understanding, and if you look for it as for silver and search for it as for hidden treasure, then you will understand the fear of the Lord and find the knowledge of God" (Proverbs 2:1-5).

Parents, the greatest legacy we can pass on to our children is not a material inheritance, or even a good name. It is a spiritual heritage, a desire we've planted in our children to walk in the way of the Lord. God will place other influential individuals in the paths of our children, but we remain the principal authorities in their lives. In many ways, we represent God to our children.

A little boy grew frightened one night during a very loud thunderstorm. He called out to his father in the next room, "Daddy, I am scared!" His father didn't want to get out of bed, so he replied, "Son, don't be scared. God is with you." The boy paused for a moment, then said, "Yeah, but I want someone with skin on right now."

In many ways, we parents are like God "with skin on" to our children. Many of the attitudes that our children develop about God will be based upon their relationship with us as a father or mother. For that reason, we all need to work hard to provide our children with a godly influence.

When our children watch how their mother and father consistently live out what they profess, they take it for granted that such a lifestyle is true and right and worthy to be emulated. They follow what they see. And *that's* a spiritual legacy that brings "no greater joy."

+ MARRIAGE BUILDER

> We all have to remember that we are not curators of the dead, we are stewards of the living. We are surrounded by the children who must move into tomorrow. Someday we will stand before the God who bought our eternal souls on the cross. Now we are leaving a legacy. Then we will give an account. Between now and then is all the time that we have left. TIM KIMMEL[70]

58

Building on the Rock

Anyone who listens to my teaching and obeys me is wise, like a person who builds a house on solid rock. Though the rain comes in torrents and the floodwaters rise and the winds beat against that house, it won't collapse, because it is built on rock. But anyone who hears my teaching and ignores it is foolish, like a person who builds a house on sand. When the rains and floods come and the winds beat against that house, it will fall with a mighty crash.
MATTHEW 7:24-27 (NLT)

THE FOUNDATION ON WHICH you build your marriage will determine its staying power. So what's the best foundation? The Bible leaves no doubt: "Unless the Lord builds the house," says Psalm 127:1, "its builders labor in vain." The proper foundation is essential.

So may I ask—is your marriage built on the Rock, or is it heading for the rocks? Is your union built upon Jesus Christ and His unchanging Word or on the shifting sands of human opinion and emotion? Your answer makes all the difference.

If your marriage is built on the Rock, then you will carefully listen to what Jesus says through the Scriptures. You will hear His words and gladly commit yourself to obey whatever He tells you. In so doing, you declare with King David, "The Lord is my rock, my fortress and my deliverer; my God is my rock, in whom I take refuge, my shield and the horn of my salvation. He is my stronghold, my refuge and my savior" (2 Samuel 22:2-3). Nothing can ultimately shake you—neither storm, flood, nor catastrophe.

On the other hand, if your marriage is not built on Christ, you will more than likely ignore His instructions, and you won't apply them to your life. You may continue to attend church services and Bible studies, but you'll feel no desire or obligation to actually *do* what Jesus says. And if that's the case, you will be like Jeshurun, who "abandoned the God who made him and rejected the Rock his Savior" (Deuteronomy 32:15).

The foundation you've chosen for your marriage will reveal itself clearly when the rains fall and the floods rise—and both *will* come. Jesus said that the rain will descend in torrents, the floodwaters will mount, and the winds will roar. Into every marriage a little rain must fall. Sometimes it's a light drizzle; at other times it's El Niño! But every marriage *will* be tested. Every marriage *will* face difficulties and surprise attacks. Our loving Savior wants us to be ready—and He says that sand just doesn't cut it as a foundation. The only safe way to survive the coming storms is to remain securely anchored to the Rock.

+   MARRIAGE BUILDER

God is the Rock who speaks to us, boldly and authoritatively, through the pages of Scripture. The Bible's words are His words. For this reason, we don't have to guess or speculate about the moral issues that confront us in the Bold New World. If we will but take the time to read and listen, the Rock has answers. ROBERT LEWIS[71]

59

NO Accident

One thing I do: Forgetting what is behind and straining toward what is ahead,
I press on toward the goal to win the prize for which God has called me
heavenward in Christ Jesus. PHILIPPIANS 3:13-14

YOU SOMETIMES HEAR IT said that a couple has "a marriage made in heaven." But what's the flip side of that? A marriage made in hell? It's as if some people believe that good marriages just sort of tumble out of the sky and that bad ones ooze up from below.

The truth, of course, lies elsewhere.

Good marriages do not "just happen." They are not the happy, unplanned result of good fortune or the fortuitous combination of pleasant genes. Good marriages take work—hard work, long work, persistent and creative work. For good reason, happy marriages sometimes get compared to successful athletic teams.

The best teams do not simply "happen." Occasionally, the managers of some professional teams appear to think that all they need to do is to collect a boatload of talent, and the championship is theirs. But almost never do such teams end up winning the big games. They may win a lot of games, but when playoff time comes and they have to face teams that have worked hard to learn how to play together as a unit, they lose. Talented groups of individuals can never consistently outperform hard-working, well-meshed teams.

And the amazing thing is, the harder these well-oiled teams work to function as a unit, the more effortless their play appears to be to observers.

Players anticipate the moves of teammates and end up scoring almost before their opponents recognize the threat. They're just fun to watch, almost as if the team were ... *made in heaven?*

But of course, it wasn't. To get to this level of excellence, team members have to put in long hours of practice together, working through problems, smoothing out conflicts, polishing roles, learning how best to encourage one another, trying new approaches.

It's really no different in marriage. Certainly God loves to partner with husbands and wives to build their marriages into loving units of championship caliber, but no good marriage is simply "made in heaven." Behind the success and the confetti and the celebration lies a whole lot of hard, determined work.

Happy couples put to work in their marriages the same mindset that drove the apostle Paul in his faith: "One thing I do: Forgetting what is behind and straining toward what is ahead, I press on toward the goal to win the prize for which God has called me heavenward in Christ Jesus" (Philippians 3:13-14).

Be sure of one thing: A happy and lasting marriage is no accident. If you see a good marriage, realize it is the result of considerable applied effort. It may not be a marriage made in heaven, but it's definitely a marriage celebrated there.

+ MARRIAGE BUILDER

I visited in an office one time where there was a sign: "In ten years what will you wish you had done today? DO IT NOW!" That's good advice for the Christian home builder. We need to form a mental image now of what we want for our home and children ten years from now. HOWARD HENDRICKS[72]

imitate God

Be imitators of God, therefore, as dearly loved children. EPHESIANS 5:1

BEFORE WE TACKLE WHAT God says specifically to wives and husbands, let's remind ourselves that both men and women are instructed to imitate the Lord. Our heavenly Father tells us to "live a life of love, just as Christ loved us and gave himself up for us as a fragrant offering and sacrifice to God" (Ephesians 5:2). The most important aspect of reflecting the character of God is to live a life of love.

Does that seem like an awfully tall order? It should! On our own, no one among us can effectively imitate God or live up to His lofty standards of love. Nevertheless, even something as extraordinary as "imitating God" lies within our reach—so long as we have anchored our lives to the Rock and are depending every moment upon His strength, not our own.

Never forget that the calling of God is the enabling of God. Whatever the Lord calls us to do, He enables us to accomplish. He never sets us up to fail; He never gives us instructions impossible to carry out.

So how can we obey His direction to imitate the Lord? The secret is found in Ephesians 5:18, where we discover the power source that makes all our obedience and all our success in marriage possible: "Be filled with the Spirit." Only as we are continuously filled with the Holy Spirit does God give us the power to do what He has called us to do.

What does it mean, in practical terms, to depend every moment on the power of the Holy Spirit? It may be as simple as breathing a quick prayer for the strength to love your spouse when you really feel like letting him or her "have it." It may mean asking God to give you the willingness to start a task or finish a household job that you really detest. It may mean pleading with the Lord to change your heart rather than demanding that He change your mate. It may mean all sorts of things—but they all boil down to inviting God to participate actively with you in building your marriage.

Naturally, "living a life of love" is a lifelong pursuit and none of us will fully "arrive" until we see the Lord face-to-face (see 1 John 3:2). Until that day, however, the Lord instructs us to "imitate God" by walking in love, just as Christ did. A tall order? Sure. But it comes with a terrific bonus package.

+ MARRIAGE BUILDER

Those who follow Christ have a much better chance at accomplishing the Bible's odd mathematics of marriage, of making two become one. Why? Because such people bring an expectation of gradual growth to their marriage. They expect time to act as their friend as they live together. Such a mind-set not only carries them past unexpected setbacks, but also gives them an assurance that added years of maturing can only better their current condition. DAVID MAINS[73]

Notes

1. A. Skevington Wood, "Ephesians" in *The Expositor's Bible Commentary*, vol. 11, ed. Frank E. Gaebelein (Grand Rapids, Mich.: Zondervan, 1978), 72.

2. Dr. Larry Crabb, *The Marriage Builder* (Grand Rapids, Mich.: Zondervan, 1992), 115.

3. Al Janssen, *The Marriage Masterpiece* (Wheaton, Ill.: Tyndale House, 2001), 69.

4. C. S. Lewis, *Mere Christianity* (New York: Macmillan, 1952), 99.

5. Ernest Hemingway, quoted in *The International Thesaurus of Quotations* (New York: HarperC, 1996), 393.

6. William Shakespeare, *The Taming of the Shrew*, in *The Complete Works of Shakespeare*, ed. David Bevington (New York: Longman, 1997), 4.1.193-96.

7. Jack and Carole Mayhall, *Marriage Takes More Than Love*, rev. ed. (Colorado Springs, Colo.: NavPress, 1996), 121.

8. Arlene Dahl, *The Quotable Woman*, ed. Carol Turkington (New York: McGraw, 2000), 116.

9. Dale Hanson Bourke, "The Real Meaning of Romance," *Today's Christian Woman*, September/October 1987, 5.

10. Bill Carmichael, quoted in William and Nancie Carmichael, *601 Quotes about Marriage & Family* (Wheaton, Ill.: Tyndale House, 1998), 99.

11. John Piper, *Desiring God,* 10th Anniversary Expanded Edition (Sisters, Oreg.: Multnomah, 1996), 179-80.

12. Ray Stedman, "Adam's Rib or Women's Lib?" *Expository Studies in First and Second Timothy* (Palo Alto, Calif.: Penin- sula Bible Church, 1981-82), catalog #3768.

13. Phil Downer, *Brave, Strong & Tender* (Sisters, Oreg.: Multnomah, 1996), 90.

14. John Piper, *A Godward Life* (Sisters, Oreg.: Multnomah, 1997), 291.

15. David DeWitt, *The Mature Man* (Gresham, Oreg.: Vision House, 1994), 123.

16. Dr. James C. Dobson, *Love for a Lifetime* (Portland, Oreg.: Multnomah, 1987), 58.

17. Crabb, *Marriage Builder,* 115.

18. Tim Stafford, *Finding the Right One* (Portland, Oreg.: Multnomah, 1985), 11.

19. Southern Baptist Convention, *Baptist Faith and Message,* section XVIII, "The Family," June 10, 1998; <www.sbc.net/bfm/bfm2000.asp#xviii>.

20. John Piper, from a wedding homily for John and Kristen Ensor, June 10, 1978.

21. Floyd McClung, Jr., *God's Man in the Family* (Eugene, Oreg.: Harvest House, 1994), 144.

22. R. C. Sproul, *The Intimate Marriage* (Wheaton, Ill.: Tyndale House, 1990), 41.

23. C. S. Lewis, *Mere Christianity,* 99.

24. Robertson McQuilkin, "Living by Vows," (Columbia, S.C.: Columbia International University, 1995?), 8; originally published in *Christianity Today,* October 8, 1990.

25. David and Karen Mains, *Living, Loving, Leading* (Portland, Oreg.: Multnomah, 1988), 102.

26. Nathaniel Branden, "Advice That Could Save Your Marriage," *Readers Digest,* October 1985, 28.

27. Mayhall, *Marriage,* 35.

28. Mains, *Living, Loving, Leading,* 67.

29. Wood, *Expositor's Bible Commentary,* 75.

30. Max Lucado, *The Final Week of Jesus* (Sisters, Oreg.: Multnomah, 1994), 22.

31. Piper, *Desiring God,* 183-84.

32. Linda Dillow, *How to Really Love Your Man* (Nashville, Tenn.: Nelson, 1993), 68-69.

33. Anne Graham Lotz, interview by Larry King, *Larry King Live,* CNN, 18 May 2000.

34. Alda Ellis, *A Gentle Beauty Within* (Eugene, Oreg.: Harvest House, 1999), 10.

35. Ibid., 62.

36. Mayhall, *Marriage,* 17.

37. Not her real name.

38. Janssen, *Marriage Masterpiece*, 47.

39. Walter Wangerin, Jr., *As for Me and My House* (Nashville, Tenn.: Nelson, 1987), 74.

40. Steve Farrar, *Point Man* (Sisters, Oreg.: Multnomah, 1990), 94.

41. Steven J. Lawson, *Men Who Win* (Colorado Springs, Colo.: NavPress, 1992), 199–200.

42. Linda Dillow and Lorraine Pintus, *Intimate Issues* (Colorado Springs, Colo.: Waterbrook, 1999), 7.

43. Dr. Ed Young, *Pure Sex* (Sisters, Oreg.: Multnomah, 1997), 23.

44. Wangerin, *As For Me*, 24.

45. *Life Application Study Bible,* note on Psalm 1 (Wheaton, Ill.: Tyndale House, 1991).

46. Barna Research Online, "Christians Are More Likely to Experience Divorce Than Are Non-Christians," December 21, 1999; <www.barna.org>.

47. Gary Richmond and Lisa Bode, *Ounce of Prevention* (Ann Arbor, Mich.: Vine, 1995), 9.

48. Steve Farrar, *Standing Tall* (Sisters, Oreg.: Multnomah, 1994), 231.

49. Aletha Jane Lindstrom, "A Legacy of Rainbows," *Focus on the Family*, April 1986, 12.

50. Ibid.

51. Gary Smalley and John Trent, *Home Remedies: Timeless Prescriptions for Today's Families* (Portland, Oreg.: Multnomah, 1991), 24.

52. Brackets are in the original text of *The Amplified Bible.*

53. Charles R. Swindoll, *You and Your Child* (Nashville, Tenn.: Nelson, 1977), 21.

54. Carolyn Kohlenberger and Noel Wescombe, *Raising Wise Children* (Portland, Oreg.: Multnomah, 1990), 41.

55. Farrar, *Standing Tall*, 215.

56. Tim Kimmel, *Legacy of Love* (Portland, Oreg.: Multnomah, 1989), 24.

57. Charles R. Swindoll, *Growing Wise in Family Life* (Portland, Oreg.: Multnomah, 1988), 112.

58. David Jeremiah, *Gifts from God* (Colorado Springs, Colo.: Victor, 1999), 92.

59. Tim Kimmel, *Homegrown Heroes* (Portland, Oreg.: Multnomah, 1990), 188.

60. Patrick M. Morley, *The Man in the Mirror* (Brentwood, TN: Wolgemuth & Hyatt Publishers, Inc., 1989), 97.

61. Sheldon and Eleanor Glueck, *Delinquents and Nondelinquents in Perspective* (Cambridge, Mass.: Harvard University Press, 1968).

62. Michael W. Smith in "My Father's Influence," *Worldwide Challenge*, May/June 1989, 35.

63. Original source unknown.

64. Tony Evans, *No More Excuses: Be the Man God Made You to Be* (Wheaton, Ill.: Crossway, 1996), 173.

65. Ken Gire, *Thanks, Dad, for Teaching Me Well* (Colorado Springs, Colo.: Waterbrook, 1999), xiii.

66. Original source unknown.

67. Herbert Hoover, quoted in *For Dad, From a Thankful Heart* (Grand Rapids, Mich.: Zondervan, 1998), 79.

68. Nicholas Wolterstorff, quoted in *For Dad,* 113.

69. John Greenleaf Whittier, "Maud Muller," quoted in John Bartlett, *A Collection of Passages, Phrases, and Proverbs Traced to Their Sources in Ancient and Modern Literature,* ed. Emily Morison Beck (Boston: Little, 1980), 513.

70. Kimmel, *Legacy of Love,* 262.

71. Robert Lewis with Rich Campbell, *Real Family Values* (Gresham, Oreg.: Vision House, 1995), 81.

72. Howard Hendricks, *Heaven Help the Home* (Wheaton, Ill.: Victor, 1973), 133.

73. Mains, *Living, Loving, Leading,* 89.